THE SANDLER® RULES

FOR SALES LEADERS

David Mattson

Sandler Training®

Paperback ISBN: 978-0-692-82133-6

E-book ISBN: 978-0-692-82240-1

This book is dedicated to the memory of David Sandler, who devoted his professional career to raising the bar for salespeople and sales leaders. He created a system that is now used by millions of people throughout the world.

The greatest gift David gave us was his selling and management rules, which allow us to think on our own and apply his powerful ideas effectively in any number of situations.

I also dedicate this book to our Sandler trainers worldwide, who have taken David's concepts to a level he would be proud of and, frankly, would never thought was possible. I have never seen a group so committed to the success of sales leaders as the hundreds of Sandler trainers around the world. It is an honor to work with them.

CONTENTS

ACKNOWLEDGMENTS

MY DEEP GRATITUDE for help on this project goes out to Bill Bartlett, Rush Burkhardt, Jerry Dorris, Gary Harvey, Troy Elmore, Elizabeth Faust, Rob Fishman, Antonio Garrido, Robin Green, Kevin Hallenbeck, Jena Heffernan, Steve Herzog, Margaret Jacks, Markku Kauppinen, Joel Kaczmarek, Hamish Knox, Dave Lebert, Colum Lundt, Joe Marr, Laura Matthews, Kayla McGee, Jim Marshall, Linc Miller, Mike Montague, Steve Montague, Rachel Miller, Heidi Pfleger, Désirée Pilachowski, Karl Scheible, Jasamine Stephens, Brian Sullivan, Susan Sykes, Steve Taback, Yusuf Toropov, David Trapani, and Lisa Von Massow.

.

Read This First

SALES LEADERSHIP IS one of the most difficult positions in any organization. It may well be *the* most difficult.

Think about it. As a sales leader, you are expected to carry out truly Herculean tasks. You have to bring revenue into the company without which the company perishes. Yet you can't possibly do that on your own. You have to do it by means of relationships with employees who are famously independent: the people on your sales team, whose performance—for better or for worse—will always reflect on you. It's your job to find those salespeople, motivate them, and coach them. At the same time, though, you've got to confirm that they're actually doing the right types of activities, day after day. That's no easy task, given the statistics. (My favorite these days is the one suggesting it typically takes over eight cold attempts to reach a single prospect.)

Now, doing all that is a pretty tall order. But the job doesn't stop there.

Sales leaders accept all that responsibility knowing full well that, typically, two out of three people on the team are not making quota and knowing, too, that most of them do not have an effective sales process to follow. Translation: They do not know on any given day what it takes for them to succeed. It's your job as sales leader to identify and help them implement that process. It's also very likely that the team does not have a strong sales culture within the organization to fall back on, a culture that will support them when they work to meet and exceed goals. It's your responsibility to create, nurture, and sustain that culture, too.

As if all of that weren't enough, you are tasked with figuring out the behavioral styles of each of your team members so you can interact with them effectively as individuals. Of course, you also need to develop and grow each member of the team over time—while simultaneously attending to your own personal and professional growth. Last but certainly not least, you need to determine the right balance when it comes to your own interactions with clients, both internal and external—a rather complex dance by itself.

Most sales managers we meet tell us there's simply not enough time to do it all, let alone do it all well. We disagree—but we also believe that time is the single most precious commodity a sales leader has. In fact, that's the main reason I wrote this book: to help you, the sales leader, make the very most of the time available to you.

THE HARD TRUTH WE TRY TO IGNORE

Here's a hard truth that too many sales leaders try to ignore: Most are expected to perform this absurdly difficult job without having received any meaningful training that supports the role you're expected to fill.

In our experience, less than 1 in 20 people responsible for leading a sales team receive the proper training to become an effective sales manager or sales leader. Typically, they're promoted into the job of sales leader on the (erroneous) assumption that the skills necessary to be a successful salesperson are the same skills necessary to be a successful leader. By default, they defer back to their sales experience. So what happens? They try to be a sales leader using the selling skills that they've mastered. They struggle—they sometimes fail.

Where do most sales leaders learn the skills, behaviors, and attitudes that actually support them in their management role? Well, they could learn from observing others in their organization or from their experience of being managed themselves. If it's the latter, they are likely to select from the things that they liked (or didn't like) back when they were a sales producer. Although this approach is common, it's not the most productive. There's no strategic approach connecting what's been experienced to what's being implemented. Like learning from watching others, it's basically trial and error—and that's a very, very expensive way for a manager to learn.

The question is, how did we at Sandler create an easy-to-read roadmap for sales leaders that respects their time and leads to success? We certainly wanted to capitalize on their experience, but we also needed to set concise, easy-to-understand guidelines about what has worked in the past and is working right now, for other sales leaders, regardless of industry. Thus: this book. That's what I've assembled here: a roadmap you can use quickly, without a lot of study ahead of time.

WHY FOLLOW THE SANDLER RULES?

Back in the late 1960s and early '70s, David Sandler—my boss and the creator of the Sandler Selling System® methodology—developed a truly revolutionary model: a consistent, workable set of rules that were reliable principles you could count on as a sales professional interested in making a good living without sacrificing either integrity or self-esteem. A lot of people don't know that these rules were initially directed to both salespeople and sales leaders. This is, in part, because in the years since, the Sandler organization has spent more time focusing on systematizing the now-famous Sandler Rules for salespeople.

The original 49 Sandler Rules have become a resource for salespeople in every major industry, all around the world, working at all experience levels. With those first 49 rules, we basically said, "These are the guiding principles that will make you successful." We didn't tell you what to say specifically during a meeting or call, but we did say what you needed to focus on internally, and we showed you how to approach certain aspects of the job in such a way as to make your job more rewarding and successful, financially and otherwise, for you and your team.

I believe those first 49 rules reached such a huge audience because they were flexible enough to allow salespeople to apply the ideas in ways that allowed them to be self-sufficient and think for themselves. The first 49 rules allowed salespeople to create their own path forward, using the guidelines of the rules as their GPS, so to speak. Is there more than one road back to your home town? Yes, there is. Is one longer than the other? Always. The point is that while there are many roads to get you there, you have to choose the best road for yourself, based on factors like traffic, weather and, yes, experience. The first book (*The Sandler Rules: 49 Timeless Selling Principles and How to Apply Them*, by yours truly) helped salespeople to chart that kind of course.

This book, *The Sandler Rules for Sales Leaders*, is meant to do the same for sales leaders. Whether you're new or experienced, these 49 rules will help you become more effective and more efficient in your day-to-day job of managing salespeople. These rules are meant to help you chart your own best path forward.

You won't find scripts or formulas here. Our experience is that, when you follow someone else's instructions word for word, it creates learned helplessness. There's no ownership of the tactics or strategies. I wrote this book using Sandler's principles as the starting point, with the goal of helping you to create your own personal playbook for sales leadership.

I believe the only "right" playbook is the one you create for yourself. You can't achieve the highest levels of success with a playbook you've inherited from someone else, a playbook that's incomplete, or a playbook with which you don't agree.

In the pages that follow, you're going to begin focusing with greater clarity on what's working (and what isn't) in terms of your behaviors, your attitude, and your technique as a sales leader. The 49 rules that follow are the basis of David Sandler's teachings for managers, going back half a century, and updated for the Information Age in which we live. Although a working knowledge of the original Sandler Rules for salespeople is helpful in putting the rules in this book into action, it's not essential.

In combination with the first book for salespeople, the 49 rules for sales leaders you're about to discover have made Sandler one of the leading training organizations in the world. I hope that you use them in the way my mentor David Sandler challenged me to use them: by making them your own.

David H. Mattson
President/CEO, Sandler Training

Use a Common Process

Are you and your team speaking the same language?

HERE'S A MYSTERY. Most departments in an organization have a common language and a common process. Everyone in Accounting talks the same language. In Marketing, there's a very analytical process by which everyone agrees to measure results. In Operations, or Engineering, or any other part of the organization you care to name, everyone agrees on the process by which the work gets done, and everyone agrees on the key terms that connect to that process. Yet Sales, for some reason, typically doesn't have a consistent process that managers and salespeople understand and agree to follow. In fact, on most sales teams, salespeople tend to resist any attempt to establish a consistent process for the team as a whole—and managers tend to let them. Why?

If you don't have a common language within the sales team, you may rationalize your way out of the problem by looking to hire veterans who bring their best practices with them. That only makes the problem worse, though, as everyone on the team begins to contribute their own best practices. Pretty soon, you find yourself leading a team that has nothing in common.

Not having a common sales process is often a contributing factor to team resistance to the customer relationship management (CRM) system. The CRM either becomes the sales process by default (a situation that carries with it any number of potential problems) or it doesn't mirror what the sales group does and therefore offers no value to the team.

Creating a common language and a common process for every sales professional in the organization (including you) seems like the kind of common-sense step every team would follow. Yet most of the sales leaders we at Sandler talk to have no shared process to use when interacting with salespeople about the most important issues, such as coaching, debriefing, onboarding, and sales-funnel management. Mutual mystification and improvisation are the default settings.

- When a salesperson tells you a meeting with a prospect "went well," do you both agree on what "went well" actually means?
- When a salesperson says that a prospect is "definitely qualified," are you sure you're both using the word "qualified" to describe the same thing?
- When a salesperson tells you that a proposal is "ready to present," do you both know with absolute certainty that the prospect's answer to the presentation is not going to be any variation on, "Let us think it over"?
- Does the salesperson know what it takes to close out the current step—and what the next step in the sales process is?

If you answered, "No," to even one of those questions, you and your team are not on the same page. Sales professionals who follow the Sandler Selling System methodology, by contrast, are consistently on the same page with each other. How can you tell if you're one of these sales professionals?

- You know that the only kind of meeting that can possibly "go well" is one that leads to a clear, scheduled next step—with an agenda that both you and the prospect have agreed on ahead of time.
- You know that prospects who are qualified meet three specific criteria: They have a pain that they are motivated to fix that you can make go away; they know what the available budget is and have discussed it with you; and they have been completely transparent with you about the decision-making process that will yield either a *yes* or a *no*. That's what "qualified" means.
- Last but not least, you know that any presentation that results in a "think it over" response is fatally flawed and should never have been given in the first place.

Managers and salespeople who follow the Sandler system consistently agree on all this and much more—because the managers have learned to follow the Sandler Rules for sales leaders.

Those rules are the subject of this book. The first rule is a pretty simple one: Make absolutely sure you and your team are using the same vocabulary and the same playbook once the game starts. That's non-negotiable. If you don't commit to this rule, sustainable positive change for you and the team is impossible.

Here's a simple test you can conduct. Bring your people together into a room. Pass out sheets of paper and pens. Ask your salespeople to write down the process they follow—from the time prospecting begins to the time the customer is buying additional products and services. Collect the sheets and compare the answers. Odds are, unless they've all been carefully trained, they will not have a similar approach.

So do the following. Have your team come up with the "big picture" steps: prospecting, qualifying, etc. Make sure everyone agrees on what these major steps are. (Your Sandler trainer can help you synchronize what you come up with to the Sandler system.) Formalize and print out the process; make sure each person on the team gets a copy. Cover all the bases:

- Prospecting
- Qualifying
- Etc.

Then, as a group, come up with two to four things that need to be accomplished within each of those steps before proceeding to the next one. Print the process out and make sure each person has a copy. Train and coach to that process.

THE SANDLER TAKEAWAY FOR SALES LEADERS

In order for you and your team to improve and take big steps forward, you must make sure that you're all speaking the same language. There are any number of good ways that you can do this, but at the very least, you should:

1. Sit your group down and decide what it is that you do, step-by-step, from the time that you prospect to the time that you're selling products and services to your client.
2. Synchronize this with the submarine model you'll learn about in the next chapter.
3. Once you've captured that, you'll be able to publish it. Then you can start to train and coach to that model.

For information on how to get Sandler's Gate Selling Tool, which will help you implement this rule, see the Appendix.

Live the Process

Reinforce your sales process until it's second nature for everyone—your team is only as strong as its weakest link.

DAVID SANDLER, THE founder of Sandler Systems, Inc., patterned his selling system after the compartments of a submarine.

Each step of the Sandler system mirrors a submarine's compartments; each must be handled in the proper order for the prospect and the salesperson to move through the sales process together. The steps of the Sandler system are:

1. **Bonding & Rapport:** Building a relationship by developing a way to communicate effectively with prospects and building trust.

2. **Up-Front Contracts:** Getting on the same page as prospects by setting expectations and ensuring a clear outcome to each sales call and each step in the sales process.

3. **Pain:** Finding prospects' reasons to buy and gaining a commitment to resolve any issues that are keeping prospects from greater success.

4. **Budget:** Determining what prospects are willing and able to invest to fix their pain.

5. **Decision:** Working with prospects' processes to make a decision on your product or service.

6. **Fulfillment:** Matching solutions to each pain uncovered during the sales process.

7. **Post-Sell:** Dealing with "buyer's remorse" and blocking competitors from reopening a sale that has closed along with securing referrals.

The Sandler system covers both strategies and tactics because it is a behavioral process map. There are specific behaviors associated with each compartment of the submarine. Those behaviors, when executed, equal results. Most managers just look at the results. They don't look at the behavior that produces the results. The submarine helps you to avoid that problem—but only if it becomes part of your sales team's culture.

In the world of enterprise selling (see Rule #31), there's a slightly different Sandler process to follow for the longer, more complex sales model you'll find there. But the Sandler system still serves as the model for each stage in that sales process.

Sandler philosophies should be part of your organization's DNA. They should guide salespeople as they talk to prospects and customers and inform managers as they talk to their salespeople. These philosophies—setting goals, creating a roadmap to get you where you want to be, monitoring your own behaviors and comparing them to daily targets, knowing it's OK to close the file, knowing that role-play makes you strong, and being accountable—can't just be slogans. They can't just be posters you hang up on the wall. They have to be the way you actually conduct business, day after day after day. They have to be how you live your sales life.

So the big question is: How do you make your sales process part of your corporate DNA? Obviously, that's not something that happens as the result of a single memo or a single meeting. Here are some ideas to consider.

- Make the sales process part of your onboarding program. Each new hire should know your process and be able to explain it. Each new hire should be tested on that knowledge.
- The sales process steps of the Sandler Submarine should be visible in graphic form from everyone's desk. People should see it every day.
- The sales process should also be built into your CRM tool. Each stage should move the CRM's close rate forward.
- Managers should use the sales process as the basis of their debriefing with salespeople. Managers should ask what happened and what's next based on the steps of the sales process and which part of the sales process should be completed next. This congruent behavior by managers is key.
- All coaching (see Rule #21) should revolve around the sales process. If managers reinforce the process, it will become part of corporate culture.
- Use the language of the system. For instance, "What's the upfront contract?" (See Rule #3.)

THE SANDLER TAKEAWAY FOR SALES LEADERS

Make a good sales process and a good selling philosophy part of your sales team's culture.

1. Integrate the sales process and its language into everything you do as a leader.
2. Find multiple ways to keep messaging about the sales process in front of the team.
3. The Sandler Submarine is a behavioral process map. It must drive your sales process and be part of the team's DNA.

No Mutual Mystification

Accountability requires clarity of expectations.

AS A MANAGER, have you ever experienced any of these issues?

- Your salespeople's calls don't seem to have clear or actionable next steps with the buyer.
- Your internal meetings don't have an agenda, and if they do, they get off track too often.
- There are no actionable next steps after sales meetings or in your sales process.
- After your team delivers a proposal, too much time passes before a decision from the buyer.
- You want to have a culture of accountability, but you don't know how to start it.

In today's world, many managers don't get to develop people the way they would like. It's harder and harder to spend quality time with all the team members so managers must make sure each interaction delivers value for everyone. This means creating structure and clarity around all interactions with the team.

Not all interactions are structured, of course. There's no need to set an agenda for a short talk in the break room about last night's ballgame. But there are times you do need guidelines to make sure that people understand why they are there, that they get a chance to put their questions on the table, and that they are clear on next steps. Being a leader makes it extremely important that you identify such interactions and ensure everyone is on the same page. Formal conversations and meetings (both internal and external) are good places to add structure in the form of something Sandler calls an "up-front contract."

The up-front contract allows salespeople to set up a roadmap for a sales meeting before the discussion begins in earnest. Basically, it sets the ground rules for the discussion to come. This concept can also be applied directly to management situations. In fact, it must become part of your sales team's culture. As the leader, you set that culture by your behavior.

Up-front contracts are mutually-agreed-upon expectations between individuals that are established before moving forward in any endeavor. In sales, when you set an up-front contract with a buyer, both of you have agreed to what will happen next, provided that a specific set of events occurs. The mechanics are more involved, but the concept is simple.

In sales management, when you and a salesperson have an up-front contract, both of you know exactly how much time has been allotted for your discussion, what questions and agendas have been shared and agreed to, what decisions need to be made, and what is supposed to happen next. Neither you nor the salesperson will be surprised later.

You both want clarity and momentum; you both want to succeed. The up-front contract keeps the topics focused and the next steps clear. That's good for both sides.

How much more effective could your team be if each and every interaction had total clarity on questions like, "Why are we here? What do we each want to talk about? What are the possible outcomes?"

Most sales teams don't address those questions before an interaction begins. They waste a lot of time and mental energy trying to figure out what the other side meant or what the other person wants. If you can clear up that mutual mystification in each conversation, you will, by default, be more productive.

Think about how nice it would be if, every time you met with your team, you and all the team members had perfect clarity about why you were there and what was happening next. Think about how nice it would be if both sides got their needs met and all the supporting next steps were clearly set and agreed to. Think of the momentum you could build. Salespeople would know what was expected and where they stood each and every step of the way—and they would take action.

When you create mutual agreement, you are establishing the ground rules not only for the discussion that is about to take place but also for the working relationship between yourself and your employees. Specifically, the contract should cover the following elements.

+ **Purpose:** "Why are we here today?"
+ **Time:** "How much time are we agreeing to allot for this meeting?"
+ **Agenda:** "What is this meeting about? What do I [as the sales leader] want to cover? What do you [the salesperson or -people] want to cover?"
+ **Outcome:** "What are the potential decisions and/or next steps we want to see to by the end of the meeting?" (You'll actually discuss this prior to starting the meeting.)

You can cover these in any order you want, as long as you touch all the bases. In practice, an up-front contract could sound like this:

Manager: Thanks for taking the time to meet today. This session will take approximately 40 minutes. I have blocked out the time. Is that still good for you as well?

Salesperson: Yes. I have set aside one hour so we are fine.

Manager: OK. Great. My feeling is that we should focus on prospecting over this period of time. What I'm hoping is that we will both contribute thoughts on ways to improve your effectiveness in this key area, and, at the end of the meeting, develop some action steps for you to take between this session and the next one. Are you comfortable with us spending our time this way?

Salesperson: Yes, I am. Sounds fine.

Manager: Is there anything you'd like to add?

Salesperson: Well, I know I'm struggling with developing a consistent prospecting methodology, and I know there are times when I avoid prospecting altogether because of that. Additionally, I'm having trouble dealing with the constant rejection I face on the phone.

Manager: OK. I'll add those issues to the list, and we can deal with them during the session.

You will find your meetings are more productive, anxiety on both sides will decrease, and goals will be met if you manage your interactions with customers and team members using up-front contracts. Contracts like these model an important selling behavior for the team, make your life easier, make your salesperson's life easier, and lead to much more productive interactions. They do require more effort and practice—but this investment in time and energy pays off many times over.

THE SANDLER TAKEAWAY FOR SALES LEADERS

Make the up-front contract part of your sales team's culture.

1. Before any meeting make sure you briefly discuss its purpose, time, agenda, and possible outcomes.
2. Use up-front contracts to set expectations for an interaction and manage by creating accountability.
3. Ask what the up-front contract will be for each call your team goes on. Use that language.

For information on how to get Sandler's Up-Front Contract Tool, which will help you implement this rule, see the Appendix.

Become a Servant Leader

Put the needs of your team first.

THE BEST SALES leaders are always checking on what they can do to help their salespeople. They know that when all the members of the team have what they need to be successful, they themselves as the managers are also successful. They take a "you-focused" approach. This approach helps them better understand the team as they interact with and support it. (By the way, the you-focused approach is also the most effective way to interact with your spouse, children, loved ones, and friends.) Sandler calls this servant leadership. It is the single best way to manage a sales team.

How do you make sure you've taken on a you-focused approach? Start by accepting two big ideas. First and foremost, your relationships with team members matter a whole lot more than your job title. Second, those relationships always depend on them believing you are serving the team.

Your goal as a sales leader must be to make sure salespeople know you have their interests at heart and will do what it takes to support them and help them succeed. After all, you win when they win.

Most traditional organizations have a hierarchal, top-down organizational chart where the person at the top says, "I am in charge—so do what I say." The most effective leaders, however, invert this chart. They say, in essence, "Hey, regardless of what the job titles say, you don't work for me. I actually work for all of you. What can I do to make your lives easier, and what can I do to support you?" In other words, they make an attitude of service to the other members of the team the cornerstone of their management style—and they mean it.

If you are comfortable in your own skin, if you are willing to do what it takes to support your team in the most effective way, then you won't be tempted to hide behind your job title or "pull rank." On the other hand, if you're not willing to support the team and you're more interested in exerting authority based on your position, the team will pick up on that—and they will lose respect for you in your role as leader. Too many managers manage with their ego rather than taking on an attitude of service. This is a big mistake. Your management role should not be where you get your ego needs met.

Your #1 job is to make sure that your individual team members are succeeding. You have to set up a plan to get that done. In setting up that plan, it's important to bear in mind that one of the many reasons people leave a company is that they don't respect their manager. Note: It's not that they don't respect the institution of management—they don't respect the specific individual.

That's not where you want to land. Think of the three people on your team you would most like to hold onto—and then start asking yourself some tough questions: How much do those people respect you, right now? Do they respect you enough to stick around for another year—or is every passing day a day that you get a little closer to losing them? Do they each know, on a personal level, that you are supporting them? If a competitor came along and tried to recruit them, what would happen?

Take a step back the next time you're inclined to give an order without any kind of consultation, issue an ultimatum, or end a sentence with, "...because I said so." That's not supporting the team. That's fixating on your own job title. This doesn't mean you don't make decisions. It means you explain the reasoning behind the decisions and get buy-in from the team.

THE SANDLER TAKEAWAY FOR SALES LEADERS

Just as buyers and customers need to be paid attention to and supported over time, salespeople need to be paid attention to and supported over time. Send all your salespeople the message that you really are there to serve them. Mean it.

1. Make sure you're paying attention to the needs of each member of your team.
2. Ask your team members directly, in one-on-one conversations, what you can do to help them succeed. Listen to the answers that come back, and do your best to take action on what you hear.
3. Avoid the temptation to use your position as a shield against criticism or as justification for decisions you make without talking to others whom those decisions affect. Managers who use their position on the organizational chart to pump up their own position or to win arguments inevitably end up losing good people they could have kept. They're leading with the title, instead of leading with the relationship.

Eliminate Miscommunication

What was said? What was heard?
Check before you respond.

YOU AS THE sales manager have to make sure each and every one of your team members feels secure. You have to make sure they are in an environment where they can excel. You want them to feel safe so they share accurate information with you. Otherwise, you can't help them. Be careful how you communicate because if you're not careful, the way you communicate can undermine those goals.

When you don't have a lot of time or patience, you can easily find yourself saying things like:

+ "I told you to..."
+ "Do what I say."
+ "You will..."
+ "Don't do that."

These are all preludes to miscommunication. As a manager, you are in the messaging business. How you say things is just as important as what you say. You need to understand how people talk to each other and how what is said is received.

When David Sandler developed the Sandler system, he relied on his understanding of transactional analysis (TA), developed by Dr. Eric Berne, as his human-relations model. Sandler realized that TA backed up his reasoning for why buyers and sellers act the way they do. To help you understand communication a little better, I want to briefly summarize TA and its application.

TA theory defines three ego states that influence our behavior: the Parent, the Adult, and the Child. You can think of these ego states as internal memory banks where childhood impressions—teachings and associated feelings—are stored. The Parent ego state contains unedited recordings of what you saw your mother, father, or other authority figures do and what you heard them say during your first five years of life. Sometimes, Parent messages were critical, judgmental, or prejudicial. For example, your mother and father told you what was right and wrong, what was good and bad, and what to do and what not to do. Those messages are referred to as Critical Parent messages. By contrast, other Parent messages were warm, comforting, supportive, and loving. Accordingly, those messages are referred to as Nurturing Parent messages.

The Child ego state is quite different. It's the emotional component of your makeup, a permanent record of your internal responses to experiences that occurred during the first five years of your life. This memory bank recorded your responses to what your parents and other authority figures said and did. In other words, while the Parent was recording what you should do, what you should say, and how you should act, the Child was recording how you felt about it. Throughout your life, those feelings may resurface when you are in situations that are similar to the ones you had as a child. For example, when you feel unfairly accused, dependent, or clumsy, those old Child recordings, just like the Parent recordings, are ready to play. Also recorded in your

Child memory bank are things like instincts, intuition, curiosity, biological urges, and a sense of physical self. So while the "have-tos" reside in the Parent ego state, the "want-tos"—urges and desires—reside in the Child ego state.

Which brings us to the third ego state, the Adult. This memory bank is all about conclusions and logic. How did it start out? Well, when you were about ten months old, you began to build understandings of your own. You were crawling, climbing, and eventually walking and exploring—taking in and processing information on your own. You began to develop your own intentions, your own explanations, and your own reasons. Back at that very early age, your Adult began storing information, which was based on logical evaluations of ideas. Unlike the Parent and Child, which stopped recording data after about five years, the Adult continues to revise and make new data entries throughout your life.

The Adult ego state is important because it acts as a referee between the demands of the Parent and the desires of the Child. It acts much like a computer, processing data from the Parent and the Child and also from what it collects. The Adult is logical, rational, and analytical. The Adult solves problems, determines probability, and makes decisions. The Adult also determines whether the Parent's data still applies and then accepts or rejects it. Similarly, the Adult updates the feelings recorded in the Child by examining them and determining if they are appropriate. The Adult doesn't replace the Parent or Child, nor does it change what is recorded there. It does, however, give you the choice not to replay data that no longer serves you.

Here are some important TA takeaways for managers.

+ Roughly 70% of management needs to come from your Nurturing Parent, 30% from your Adult, and 0% from your Critical Parent or your Child.

- The Nurturing Parent listens, provides positive feedback, gives compliments, and looks for the good in experiences. Sales leaders need the Nurturing Parent for effective coaching, debriefing, meetings, and even casual conversation.
- The Adult disengages from emotions and focuses on facts and experiences without moral judgment. Sales leaders use the Adult for meaningful reality-check moments—as in, "How close are you to the monthly target for X behavior?" etc.
- The Critical Parent is judgmental, talks down to people, and is not a good listener. If you're looking for a quick, effective test of whether something you plan to say is coming from your Critical Parent, ask yourself this question: "Can I picture myself saying this while pointing a finger at the salesperson?" If the answer is *yes*, think twice before you use those words.
- The Child ego state is all about wants and needs and may use strong emotion to express them. This is not the state you want to be in during discussions with salespeople. There are some intriguing varieties of the Child ego state of which managers should be aware:
  - ◇ Rebellious Child is the one who gets defensive and pushes back: "No, I won't!"
  - ◇ Adaptive Child is the one who reacts to the surrounding world around him by changing (adapting) feelings and behavior.
- Understand that your people will be in different states at different times. Your job is to look for the reasons behind why people act and say what they do. Move beyond who's right and who's wrong, who's the boss and who's the employee. Become an investigator; start checking the *why* behind the *what*. You will find that your people are open books—if you are willing to learn to read.

Acting like a leader means consciously setting aside your own Child ego state in your interactions with salespeople (or anyone else, for that matter), avoiding Critical Parent messages altogether, and choosing to communicate through Nurturing Parent and Adult messages. This takes practice. This principle also applies to the members of your sales team during their interactions with customers and buyers.

David Sandler used to tell salespeople to "leave your Child in the car" when they went out to meet with buyers. He meant that there was no place for the Child ego state during the selling process. The same applies to your interactions with your team. Take a moment before you speak. Identify what was just said. Respond in a way that supports the team.

THE SANDLER TAKEAWAY FOR SALES LEADERS

Only communicate by using your Nurturing Parent and Adult.

1. The Child ego state is counterproductive in your discussions with members of the sales team. Steer clear of it. That means no complaining, no backbiting, and no blaming—even if (especially if) a salesperson engages in these activities.
2. Think twice before engaging in "good/bad" "right/wrong" (Critical Parent) messaging. It may backfire.
3. Focus on Nurturing Parent messages ("You always give it your best shot") and logical Adult messages and questions ("What would happen if we tried...?").

Create Self-Sufficiency

Don't fix—explore.

SALES LEADERS SOMETIMES fall into the habit of solving problems for their people. I call this "superhero" mode.

Superheroes can handle anything. They can't be hurt by bullets. They can leap tall buildings in a single bound. They usually have X-ray vision. They fix and they rescue. Superheroes are there to save the day.

When presented with a sales situation from a salesperson, most managers jump right to "do this, do that." They throw on their capes and become superheroes. They rescue. They solve. All too often, they jump in too soon. They might do these things for many reasons; maybe there's a time crunch, or perhaps, at some level, they miss the old days when they were out in the field selling. It may also make an ego or two feel good to be in charge and to look like they know all the answers.

These aren't good enough reasons to go into superhero mode. Why? Because ultimately, you want your salespeople to become self-sufficient and successful. You want them to learn how to think and react to circumstances and to learn from the situations they face. When your people learn new things for themselves, they create new "muscle memory," making it second nature (see Rule #26). When you fix things for them, they don't.

If you jump in and tell people what to do, you're not always acting in their best interest even though you may tell yourself otherwise. It's easy to convince yourself that this instance is an exception—an emergency situation. But if you're honest with yourself, you'll admit that you are actually OK with the emergency and concede that, at some level, you are actually glad that it came up. Managers can love the superhero part of the job. It's better than filling out reports, and it gets them back into the interactive problem-solving mode they miss.

However, the superhero approach doesn't serve the team. If you get into the habit of putting on the cape and rescuing, you won't be helping your team members to grow. They'll stop thinking for themselves and look to you for the answer every time they face a problem.

Instead of going into superhero mode when you face a challenge, what if you were to get better at asking questions like these?

- "If you couldn't find me, how would you solve this?"
- "If someone asked you the same question, what would you tell them?"
- "Why don't you share your thoughts on this, and I can give you feedback?"

It may seem easier and quicker to solve problems for your team, but exploring the issues together and helping them to become self-sufficient will save you more time in the long run (see Rule #47). Ask your people to come up with a proposed solution to share with you, and then use this as an opportunity to coach and foster growth.

THE SANDLER TAKEAWAY FOR SALES LEADERS

Every once in a while, show vulnerability when interacting with the members of your sales team by asking for their input.

1. Resist the temptation to solve every problem.
2. When salespeople come to you for the answer to an issue, ask questions like, "How would you solve this?" Teach them to come to you prepared with possible solutions to their problems.
3. Exploring issues together and helping salespeople become self-sufficient will save you more time in the long run.

Avoid the Drama Triangle

Don't play games.

DRAMA IS GREAT on television and in movies, but if you're a sales leader it's a game you can't possibly win.

To understand why, consider the Drama Triangle, a social model created by Dr. Stephen Karpman. Karpman was a student of Dr. Eric Berne, founder of transactional analysis (see Rule #5). He used this triangle model to clarify what really takes place in drama-focused interactions:

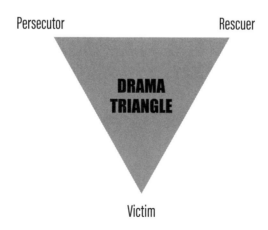

The games that take place within the Drama Triangle create a ripple effect on your team that is both profound and highly demotivating. To understand these games, notice that Karpman's three-sided figure represents three roles that arise in an unproductive personal or professional conflict: persecutor, rescuer, and victim.

The rules of this game are pretty simple. Two parties cannot be in the same corner at the same time.

- The **persecutor** begins from the position, "You have done something wrong, and I am going to let you know about it," or, "It's all your fault." The persecutor is controlling, blaming, critical, and oppressive.

- The **victim** begins from the position, "Poor me." Victims are powerless, helpless, ashamed, and unable to solve problems or challenges for themselves. Sometimes people live in the victim state full time; sometimes they are there situationally. In this position the real issue is that they don't take responsibility for their decisions or for what they could have done better. They don't learn or grow since they are stuck in the blame game. They often seek out rescuers and even persecutors.

- The **rescuer** begins from the position, "I'll save you." Rescuers typically feel guilty if they don't find some way to rescue. Rescuing keeps the victim dependent and, all too often, conveys permission to fail.

If you choose to play one or more of these recurring roles, you will find the cycle of drama perpetuating itself. It is also important to note that the Drama Triangle is a situational game. People don't consciously seek out this game, but they can easily find themselves playing it in response to the situations they face. Some people become so accustomed to the Drama Triangle that they don't know any different way to operate. When management plays the drama game, it is a sign of a lack of accountability within the department and underdeveloped coaching skills (see Rule #21). Note that the Drama Triangle is impossible to play once you create a mutually respectful relationship with the salesperson.

How does such a game play out on the sales team? There are countless variations. Here's one:

Imagine a situation where a salesperson comes to you and says, "I'm in way over my head. I've been under a lot of pressure at home, and I really need some support. Could you please help me close this account?"

You agree to go on this sales call when normally that would not be part of your role on a call. You've just become the rescuer.

If the deal doesn't close, the salesperson may move into the victim corner of the triangle and say, "I had that deal to the finish line. I needed your help. What happened? It's all your fault!"

In response, you of course move into the persecutor role by saying, "Hang on, you're the one who asked me to help with the account, remember?" or "This opportunity had no chance of closing anyway." Either is likely to perpetuate the drama, causing the game to continue on from there.

The only way to win this game is to not play it in the first place. In the situation above, what would happen if you were to respond to the salesperson's first request like this?

"Before I answer that, do you mind if I ask you a question? What would you do about this deal if, for some reason, I wasn't available? If I was sick or something like that? How would you handle this?"

A question like that, posed from the Adult ego state, takes you out of the Drama Triangle and opens up a whole new realm of possibility that includes growth and opportunity for the salesperson.

You can easily be seen as a persecutor when you challenge salespeople about their activity or level of success. The best way to avoid this is to have a daily behavioral action plan for success, what Sandler refers to as a "cookbook" (see Rule #11). This plan lets a salesperson know what specific behaviors are required for success. When you review the cookbook, you're simply following up and reinforcing behaviors rather than persecuting.

THE SANDLER TAKEAWAY FOR SALES LEADERS

The key to avoiding the Drama Triangle is to notice when you are about to be pulled into it.

1. Create strategies for breaking out of the game once you identify it. Learn to use Adult ego state questions to disengage.
2. Keep in mind that the Drama Triangle is impossible to play once you create a mutually respectful relationship with the salesperson.
3. When management is playing the drama game it is a sign of an organization where there is no accountability and where coaching skills are underdeveloped (see Rule #21).

See Your People through Their Lens

Use DISC to understand how you and your people view the world—so you can lead more effectively.

SALES LEADERS NEED to be flexible in their communication style. They have to understand that each team member sees and filters the world differently. They must understand how team members communicate and process information and what motivates them.

Have you ever noticed that some people jump to quick conclusions, often without having essential information? That others, first and foremost, want to make and keep friends? That still others don't like change and conflict and want to avoid it at any cost? Have you ever noticed that there are even some people who want all the details before they act—and may even suffer from the "paralysis of analysis"?

If you've ever noticed anyone who fit those descriptions—and I'm certain you have—then you're in a perfect position to implement this Sandler Rule. Once you understand how team members operate, you will have the key to unlocking their potential.

The DISC behavioral model is an important tool that can help you develop a much deeper understanding of the members of your sales team, buyers, and anyone else you may happen to run into during the day. An understanding of DISC is, to put it bluntly, invaluable. DISC outlines four sets of behavioral characteristics that describe, with remarkable accuracy, how human beings process information and emotion and how they prefer to interact with others.

As you may have guessed, DISC is an acronym. "D" stands for Dominant. "I" stands for Influencer. "S" stands for Steady Relator. "C" stands for Compliant. Each collection of characteristics is referred to as a behavioral style.

HOW TO IDENTIFY

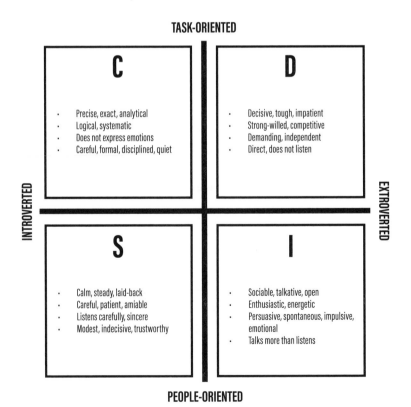

TASK-ORIENTED

C
- Precise, exact, analytical
- Logical, systematic
- Does not express emotions
- Careful, formal, disciplined, quiet

D
- Decisive, tough, impatient
- Strong-willed, competitive
- Demanding, independent
- Direct, does not listen

INTROVERTED   EXTROVERTED

S
- Calm, steady, laid-back
- Careful, patient, amiable
- Listens carefully, sincere
- Modest, indecisive, trustworthy

I
- Sociable, talkative, open
- Enthusiastic, energetic
- Persuasive, spontaneous, impulsive, emotional
- Talks more than listens

PEOPLE-ORIENTED

No one is exclusively one of the four DISC styles. Most people have a dominant or preferred main style plus one or two supporting styles depending on the person they're dealing with and the particular situation. No style is better than another. There is no "good," "bad," "right," or "wrong" style.

When you become familiar with these styles, you will begin to see others differently and appreciate those differences. DISC can help you understand how your buyers like to communicate, make decisions, and buy and how you can build a presentation that matches your buyers' preferred styles.

It's important to understand your own primary DISC style also. Once you do, you can adapt your behavior to each of the styles, and you will exponentially increase the effectiveness of communication to your salespeople—and anyone else.

- **Dominants:** Dominants are extroverted, often opinionated people who need to take action. They like to be in charge of situations. When they aren't in control, they are uncomfortable. They are bored if they aren't challenged. Dominants do not like small talk. They like to win and get ahead. They are not natural team players, but they are organized, direct, and to the point. They don't want to hear the *why*—just the *what*. Get to the point and cut the social stuff with Dominants.

- *What to watch for:* If you are a Dominant, remember to give people time to talk through things. Let people self-discover; don't just jump in and give them the answer. Try to have more patience when dealing with others.

- **Influencers:** Influencers are personable and trusting. They like to talk, interact, and leave the action to others. Since they want to be liked, they are eager team players. Influencers are creative and humorous, but are also disorganized. They can be impulsive and intuitive, relying on feelings, but they are not logical decision makers.

- *What to watch for:* If you are an Influencer, you will want to make sure you let others talk as well. Try to stay with the agenda and get clear on the next steps arising from the interaction.

- **Steady Relators:** Steady Relators are amiable, patient people who know how to keep the peace and avoid conflict. Since they practice and prefer constancy and consistency, they don't like changes or surprises. They are deliberate and can appear slow to make decisions. Steady Relators are loyal, with long-term commitments. They don't often reveal their true feelings.

- *What to watch for:* If you are a Steady Relator, the areas to watch for include: making sure you set agendas out front prior to meetings so you and others are prepared; brainstorming with a clear path forward; and making sure you share what you're thinking with your most important allies. That last one may be difficult because it's not your nature, but you do need to find a way to let people you trust know where you stand.

- **Compliants:** Compliants are cautious thinkers. Detail-oriented perfectionists, their high standards follow the book. Since they are busy getting one more fact in search of the perfect answer, they may be slow, or even unwilling, to commit to a course of action. Compliants are analytical and orderly in their thinking and acting, relying totally on facts and figures.

- *What to watch for:* If you're a Compliant, you will want to make a point of: taking time to socialize and get to know your team; systemizing what you do so you can capture best practices for others; and having a cookbook in place (see Rule #11) for yourself and others.

HOW TO COMMUNICATE

TASK-ORIENTED

C

- Use data and facts
- Examine an argument thoroughly
- Keep on task; do not socialize
- Disagree with the facts, not the person
- Use proven ideas and data
- Don't touch
- Don't talk about personal issues
- Explain carefully

D

- Be direct, brief, and to the point
- Focus on the task
- Use a results-oriented approach
- Ensure they win
- Use a logical approach
- Touch on high points and big ideas
- Don't touch; keep your distance
- Don't be emotional
- Act quickly, they decide fast

INTROVERTED

EXTROVERTED

S

- Be patient, build trust
- Draw out their opinions
- Relax; allow time for discussions
- Show how solutions affect people
- Clearly define all areas
- Involve them in planning
- Slow down your presentation
- Provide information needed
- Secure commitment step-by-step

I

- Allow time for socialization
- Lighten up; have fun
- Ask for feelings and opinions
- Use touch: forearm and back
- Be friendly and warm
- Set aside time for chatting
- Let them speak
- Give recognition
- Speak about people and feelings

PEOPLE-ORIENTED

DO'S AND DONT'S

TASK-ORIENTED

C	**D**
DO: • Give detailed information • Answer questions patiently • Give time to think and decide DO NOT: • Keep information to yourself • Pressure for immediate decisions • Be too chatty	DO: • Give immediate feedback • Concentrate on subject • Maintain result-orientation DO NOT: • Get frustrated at their desire to take action • Restrict their power • Spend time on non-essentials
S	**I**
DO: • Slow down, take your time • Provide assurance and support • Give enough time to decide DO NOT: • Be restless, pressure for action • Make sudden changes • Fail to deliver on promises	DO: • Show enthusiasm, smile, chat • Focus on the positive, have fun • Let them talk DO NOT: • Put down their enthusiasm • Focus on the details • React negatively

INTROVERTED — EXTROVERTED

PEOPLE-ORIENTED

Here's a summary of the best ways to interact with the salespeople who report to you, based on the person's dominant DISC style. Post it somewhere you can see it each day.

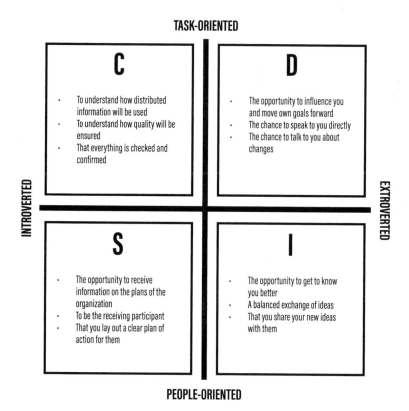

WHAT SUBORDINATES WITH THESE DISC STYLES WANT

TASK-ORIENTED

C
- To understand how distributed information will be used
- To understand how quality will be ensured
- That everything is checked and confirmed

D
- The opportunity to influence you and move own goals forward
- The chance to speak to you directly
- The chance to talk to you about changes

INTROVERTED

EXTROVERTED

S
- The opportunity to receive information on the plans of the organization
- To be the receiving participant
- That you lay out a clear plan of action for them

I
- The opportunity to get to know you better
- A balanced exchange of ideas
- That you share your new ideas with them

PEOPLE-ORIENTED

THE SANDLER TAKEAWAY FOR SALES LEADERS

The DISC behavioral model will help you understand and communicate more effectively with your team—and everyone else.

1. You must know and acknowledge how you interpret the world. You can then understand how you communicate and behave, which is the first step to being flexible with your team.

2. When you can adapt your behavior to each of the styles, you will exponentially increase the effectiveness of your communication. Profile your people so you can talk to them in their language.

3. Learn to identify the various DISC styles; learn the "do's and don'ts" associated with each.

For information on how to get Sandler's DISC Tool, which will help you implement this rule, see the Appendix.

Don't Get Smoked at the Interview

SEARCH for the right candidate.

WHEN SALES LEADERS have an opening to fill, most have to back-fill the production from the territory themselves until they locate a new salesperson. This causes them to have to do multiple jobs, which is something they can't sustain for long. Most don't hire often enough and don't make it second nature to be in recruiting mode. Managers tend to wait until their backs are against the wall—at which point they tend to abandon any hiring process they have in place.

This is a mistake. The time it takes to find the right person far outweighs hiring the wrong person and dealing with a bad hire. But sales managers train themselves not to notice that.

The people you hire are ambassadors of your brand. You need to make sure you hire the very best people, and you need to do your best to see to it that those people stick around. When good salespeople leave the team, it's disruptive and costly. No one has a budget line-item called "turnover," but companies should think about adding it. It typically costs five times a salesperson's salary to make a bad hire, after you take the manager's time into account.

The remedy is actually a simple one: Recruit with a particular profile of a salesperson in mind, and disqualify all who don't match the profile. This makes far more sense than trying to force a candidate you like into the specifics of the job in question and seeing how well the person matches up once you've made the hire.

Managers often tell themselves they're looking for the "right type of salesperson." They say, "I know the real thing when I see it." And: "I go with my gut." Accordingly, their purpose in interviewing candidates is to determine things such as: whether or not they like and can interact easily with the person; whether the person fits in with their own style as a manager; whether the person is likely to get along with the rest of the team.

There's nothing wrong with any of those criteria, but they shouldn't be your reason to hire a salesperson. They should be tiebreakers. The reason to make the hire is that the salesperson fits the profile. Without knowing what type of salesperson will actually succeed at the job, candidates can look better and better as time goes on in the hiring process and the pressure of keeping the territory viable becomes more intense. That's what leads to bad hires.

We at Sandler urge sales leaders to beware of using as their primary recruiting tool, "What does my gut say?" That's a tactic that may lead to you getting smoked at the interview. You don't want to be swept off your feet by false appearances during the interview only to be sadly disillusioned with the real person who shows up for work each day. To avoid that outcome, use the SEARCH model to develop a clear hiring profile for this position.

- **S:** What **skills** are needed to make sure this person is 100% successful? For instance, the skill of reaching out to CEOs that haven't been spoken to before and setting up both first and second meetings with them, either virtually or in person. Salespeople either know how to do something like that, or they don't. There are multiple skills people have to master to sell for your organization. Is there hard evidence that the person possesses the skills in question? What does that evidence look like?

- **E:** What **experience** is needed to make sure this person is 100% successful? For instance, one or more years of selling comparable products and services in a comparable or identical industry. How about experience in prospecting? Familiarity with earning commissions? Readiness to call on your type of buyers? Think about what experience the person would need to match up to the job you're trying to fill.

- **A:** What **attitude** is needed to make sure this person is 100% successful? How does this person self-evaluate? How does this person feel about the markets you serve? About any prior companies of employment? How do you know? Bear in mind that the attitude that is on display during the interview with you may not be the person's daily attitude toward work, peers, and management. Look for hard evidence. Do a behavioral assessment; Sandler can help you pick out the right one to use. Talk to past employers.

- **R:** What **results** are needed to make sure this person is 100% successful? If you need a hunter, then ask for hunter results. For example, about net new accounts—find out how these accounts were cultivated. What percentage of current accounts do you want to see that the person has renewed? How many accounts do you want to see up-sold?

- **C:** What **cognitive skills** are needed to make sure this person is 100% successful? Every sales job has different requirements on this front. You should know the specifics and know how this individual matches up to them. Again, do an assessment.

* **H:** What **habits** are needed to make sure this person is 100% successful? For instance, the habit of doing that whole reaching-out-to-CEOs thing mentioned in skills. The fact that someone knows how to execute a given skill doesn't necessarily make the skills a predictable behavior that supports your sales process. Does this person have the daily muscle memory that allows effective execution on the skills in question? How do you know? Here again, a behavioral assessment can save you a lot of trouble and expense.

The key is to get ahead of the curve so you've always got a good pool of candidates to choose from and you've always got people in development who are moving ahead in their careers. Use the SEARCH model to build your bench at each level.

THE SANDLER TAKEAWAY FOR SALES LEADERS

Hiring mistakes are expensive. Avoid them by using the SEARCH model.

1. Use the SEARCH model to figure out where a candidate actually fits against a job with parameters you've identified. Do the work up front and you will save yourself time, money, effort, and aggravation later.

2. Find out whether this person fits the job for which you are hiring. Don't match a good person with the wrong job.

3. Use the SEARCH model to build your bench at each level so you have lots of talent from which to choose.

For information on how to get Sandler's SEARCH Tool, which will help you implement this rule, see the Appendix.

Treat a Job Interview Like a Sales Call

Your job is to disqualify.

LET'S FACE IT—MOST managers find themselves interviewing candidates for sales positions only sporadically, when a position needs to be filled, and usually in parallel with covering as salesperson themselves for the open position. What does this situation cause? It puts the manager in "hurry up" mode, likely more desperate to fill the position than candidates are to get the job, and not as well-prepared with a complete plan for identifying, interviewing, and hiring the right person.

Never having been trained to use a successful interviewing process, most managers find themselves shooting from the hip and conducting the interview by telling candidates all about the company and the position to be filled. Although this may seem logical and is certainly acceptable, it doesn't take much for candidates to digest the information and respond in a manner that makes them seem like the perfect fit.

Prior to conducting any interviews, managers should create a job profile. This is an inventory of what will be required at the job: calling on C-level executives, making cold calls, selling net new buyers, and so on. Then, managers should match the job profile to a specific person. We recommend the SEARCH model (see Rule #9).

The Sandler Selling System methodology can be a model for handling the interviewing process more effectively. Establishing some bonding and rapport at the start of the interview is key; however, managers should be observers at that point to see if candidates have the ability to build rapport quickly. Establishing an up-front contract, which includes being able to ask and answer questions and the candidates' agreement to say "yes" or "no" at the end of the interview—should you choose to make an offer—is key to qualifying or disqualifying candidates. Why would you ever want to hire people for a sales position if they couldn't be definitive about responding to an offer? How could you expect them to get prospects to make a commitment? Initially, the managers' job is to disqualify candidates.

If the candidate makes it past the up-front contract, the focus turns to getting the candidate to do 70% of the talking by using questions to determine whether they have what you need from the SEARCH model (see Rule #9). Now you're prepared to discover whether a candidate meets the criteria for the job.

What can managers gain from a pre-planned job profile and questions for the candidate?

1. A process consistent with the sales process that new salespeople will be using once they have the job.
2. A process that is time efficient and works to get the best fit as opposed to the fastest find for the position.
3. A more competent and confident manager when it comes to filling sales positions.
4. Better hires, which lead to lower turnover.

THE SANDLER TAKEAWAY FOR SALES LEADERS

Treat interviews with job candidates like sales calls. Know what you're going to ask ahead of time, and encourage candidates to do most of the talking. You want to learn a lot about applicants in a very short amount of time—and quickly disqualify people who don't match up with the job requirements.

1. Create a job profile first so you can match the best person using the SEARCH model. Create good questions for the interview ahead of time that focus on skills, experience, attitude, results, cognitive abilities, and habits.

2. You shouldn't be selling the position. You should be disqualifying people who don't match the profile.

3. Outline your hiring process and follow it.

Manage Behavior, Not Results

Create a recipe for success.

MANY LEADERS MANAGE their salespeople by managing the numbers. They set a quota, make sure everyone knows what the quota is, and push for that quota to be hit. They track the number of sales completed, and then they try to hold the salespeople accountable by requiring status reports showing the potential for closing and estimated dates for each prospect.

There's a problem with this approach. While you can track numbers, you can't actually manage them any more than you can manage the weather.

Sure, managers keep score by revenue—it's true. The problem is, most salespeople don't have a path to get to the numbers. Numbers are the *what*. However, as a manager, you need to help your salespeople get to the *how*.

Here's an example, based on a real-life situation, that will illustrate what I mean:

Tony was given a quota of $5 million per year. Early in the year, he met with his manager Elsa, who asked if he understood the number and needed any help. Tony said he didn't need help.

Well, he couldn't have been more wrong. The real issue was that Tony didn't know how he was going to get the $5 million from his territory. Sure, he knew he needed 50 buyers. But here's what he didn't know:

- What was the right balance of new buyers compared to Tony up-selling existing customers?
- How many new conversations did he need each week?
- How many first calls did he need to make each day?

Sure, Tony was going to work hard; it just wasn't going to be smart. Without the answers to the above questions, Tony's way was going to require some luck on his side in order to hit his goal. Since that luck did not come his way in the first weeks of the first quarter, Tony found himself falling further behind his goal as time went on, and he found it demotivating and downright depressing.

Fortunately, Elsa saw what was happening and re-engaged with Tony. The solution was for Tony to identify the behaviors needed to succeed and for him to have a daily "cookbook" to follow to turn those goals into reality.

Sandler's Cookbook for Success is a set of controllable actions that, when undertaken daily, weekly, and monthly, deliver a predictable, measurable outcome that you as manager and the salesperson both agree constitutes sales success. Following a behavior plan, as outlined in a Cookbook for Success (similar to a recipe in a food cookbook), will yield the results that move the salespeople toward the agreed-upon goal. The establishment and use of a cookbook can help new salespeople and those with less experience have success similar to that of your top producers—and it's the manager's responsibility to help team members create and follow a cookbook especially designed for them as individuals.

Tony, armed with a clearer sense of his targets for new and existing business and a cookbook that Elsa helped him develop in support of those goals, was able to define the correct balance of activities he needed to do each week. He was then in control of his own behavior—the only item he could control in his journey to closing more business.

The cookbook was not only good for Tony's numbers—it was good for his head. Each day that he succeeded in meeting his behavioral goal, he had a victory to celebrate in knowing where he was on his sales roadmap—what action he had to take next, when he had to do it, and how he was going to go about it.

You must help your salespeople work back from the overall sales goal numbers to specific, controllable behaviors that will generate the desired results, thus managing the behavior, not the results.

Three big lessons stand out here. First and foremost, understand the value of managing behavior. Second, manage the cookbook for each and every member of your team. Third, have a cookbook for yourself as a sales leader. There are so many things you need to do in order to be successful; don't assume you can do this all by instinct. Identify each and every action item and decide on the frequency of each item. Once you've done that, you will know the *what*, the *how*, and the *when* of activities such as coaching team members (see Rule #21), role-play (see Rule #26), and weekly individual meetings (see Rule #37).

THE SANDLER TAKEAWAY FOR SALES LEADERS

Change the focus from managing the outcomes to managing the behavior that produces those outcomes.

1. Set number goals and then convert the goals into the behaviors needed to succeed. Create a list of behaviors and then determine how often and when those behaviors need to be carried out.
2. New salespeople and those with less experience can have the success of your top producers if you help them create and follow the right cookbook.
3. Don't forget to create a cookbook for yourself.

For information on how to get Sandler's Cookbook for Success Tool, which will help you implement this rule, see the Appendix.

Manage Individuals; Lead the Team

There's no substitute for personal attention.

MOST CEOS AGREE that in today's leaner, hypercompetitive business environment, sales managers are more pressed for time than ever. Sales managers are managing more and more people, which makes it harder and harder to give each member of the team the support needed to succeed.

Managers know that the people on the sales team need support, and they know they're not able to provide enough support. As a result, managers get stressed and frustrated. Salespeople are also spread too thin, and managers pick up on this. (Sometimes customers do, too.) All this leads to managers knowing their people need to adjust and do something different to be more efficient. So what do they do?

Managers typically believe they have three options. They can send a memo, they can call a meeting, or they can do both—hold a meeting and then summarize in a memo. The goal in all three cases is the same: Deal with all the outstanding issues the team faces by communicating with and managing issues with the team as a whole. The typical message sounds something like: "Hey there, folks—we are way behind our target and we have only four months to make that up so everybody is going to need to pitch in. I want everyone to up their prospecting numbers by 10% this week. We can do it! You rock! Call me if you need me."

How often does that actually work? Hardly ever.

Even if the numbers start to pick up, it certainly isn't because the members of the sales team were inspired by the group memo or meeting. If there is a turnaround, it is usually due to the actions of individual team members—not the actions of the manager who made the mistake of trying to coach the team in a group. There's no such thing as effective group coaching; all effective sales coaching takes place one-on-one. (See Rule #21.)

As an analogy, suppose you're a parent who has five kids and you call them together for a meeting. Assume that in that meeting, you give them all the same exact message and you communicate to all five kids as though they were identical. How well do you imagine that is going to work? Each will perceive the message differently based on their age, experience, and belief in the importance of the instructions. You've got five different young people at different ages, with different needs, goals, and personality types. They'll all likely come away from the meeting with a different understanding of the message. It's the same with a sales team.

This need to connect with each person on a team as an individual is critical to effective coaching. To be an effective coach, managers must religiously allocate one-on-one time and must be intentional about getting to know each team member individually.

Coaching is not a one-size-fits-all proposition. New hires, first-anniversary people, and veteran sales representatives have completely different knowledge levels, skills, and abilities. Managers must adjust their coaching to meet the needs of each unique individual in whatever stage of development. If individually coaching each of your team members seems challenging and maybe even a little intimidating, consider it to be sales management physics. You can get mad at the law of gravity if you want, but in the world you live in, an apple that you let go of in mid-air drops to earth—not just sometimes but all the time. It's the same with the need to individually coach team members. There's simply no way to motivate them by sending them all the same email or giving them all the same speech or calling them into a room and trying to teach them all the same technique. They will each need your individual attention. That's the reality.

The good news is that once you do make the decision to communicate with each individual salesperson as an individual—even if you think, initially, that you don't have time to do so—you will end up winning back hours in your working day. Coaching team members one-on-one breeds more personal accountability, initiative, and self-reliance. You will spend less time putting out fires that salespeople are perfectly capable of putting out themselves, and you will become aware of impending crises before they happen. You will be doing your job. See also Rule #37, which will help you set up weekly individual meetings.

THE SANDLER TAKEAWAY FOR SALES LEADERS

Only focus on coaching individuals. Coach them in private. Don't try to coach the team as a whole. There is a net time benefit to doing this. Focusing on the individual allows you to win back hours in your working day. (See Rule #21 for more information on how coaching works.)

1. Invest the time. Get to know what makes each individual member of your team tick.

2. If you focus on managing individual behaviors, the team results will reflect the progress that individual salespeople make.

3. Individuals can accept personal accountability to pursue a goal. Teams can't. (See also Rule #37, which will help you set up weekly individual meetings.)

Be a Comfort-Zone Buster

Make sure there's no room at Complacency Inn.

HAVE YOU EVER encountered salespeople who perform at or above quota for a very long stretch of time—months or even years—and then, for no apparent reason, hit a stage in their career where the numbers start to slip? Or they knock themselves out to get to a certain number and then seem to coast? What's going on there?

Sometimes people who had previously pushed themselves to succeed, day after day, week after week, quarter after quarter, begin to coast. This may happen gradually. They may not even be aware that they're doing it. Unless their managers are tracking behaviors (as opposed to simply tracking revenue, the end result), they may not be aware of what's happening until it's too late to avoid a major spiral.

There are many possible reasons for this performance pattern. One is complacency. People may simply have gotten accustomed to a steadily less-demanding comfort zone in terms of their daily activity—without realizing what the real-world consequences of such a comfort zone are likely to be. For instance, they may have lost their sense of urgency about prospecting because they've talked themselves into believing that they have enough current or repeat business to justify a certain income level. When they finally realize they don't, you've got a crisis on your hands. How do you, the manager, deal with this situation? You start by making sure the person has a good cookbook.

As discussed in Rule #11, a cookbook is a set of actions that, when undertaken daily, delivers a predictable, measurable outcome that you and the salesperson both agree constitutes sales success. This is especially helpful for long-time salespeople who find themselves coasting.

Working together, you and the salesperson must develop and use a new cookbook to establish what's most likely to happen over the next week, month, or quarter. Maybe this salesperson hasn't ever done this before, and working back from the revenue number to the behaviors will be eye-opening. Very often, this is enough to take care of complacency.

A personalized cookbook is great for busting comfort zones. It allows you to focus on small, incremental steps—as opposed to big, swooping changes. It makes it possible for both you and the salesperson to celebrate success more often since you're watching activities and not just closed sales. It helps the salesperson get motivated to retrain that muscle memory that, once upon a time, delivered the numbers that supported the income goal—back before complacency kicked in.

As I say, this is one of the easier situations for a sales leader to deal with—as long as you are committed to understanding, helping, and supporting the salesperson as an individual. All you're doing is facilitating a reality check, discussing its consequences, and then assisting the salesperson in following the cookbook you've both worked together to create. More complex scenarios include salespeople who plateau at a certain level when you know they have the potential to grow beyond that or who are, for whatever reason, afraid of success. Getting to the bottom of these issues requires a good series of ongoing coaching discussions. (See Rule #21.)

THE SANDLER TAKEAWAY FOR SALES LEADERS

Sometimes, salespeople who once pushed hard can start to slip. Many of them don't even realize that that's what they're doing. It's your job to notice when that's taking place, and the only way you can do that is to know what's going on with each member of the team.

1. Work with the salesperson to create a cookbook—a daily action plan for success.

2. Track behaviors, not just outcomes. This will help you identify situations where the salesperson's activity does not support the income goal.

3. You will need to implement a good coaching process to get to the bottom of situations where the comfort zone is based on deep-seated beliefs or behavior patterns that don't support the salesperson.

Risk Failure to Achieve Growth

"I"-10s learn from failure.

THIS ONE THROWS a lot of sales leaders—the idea that failure leads to success.

We are serious, though. It is OK to fail. Specifically, it is OK for your salespeople to fail. In fact, there's no way for them to learn and grow if they don't fail.

Think back to your own experience of, say, learning to ride a bicycle. Odds are, the very first time you got on a two-wheeler and started peddling, you didn't glide forward smoothly and easily. You didn't reach your destination without trouble, hop off, and raise your arms in triumph. No. You fell off the bike—and not just once. You fell off over and over again. Face it. You failed! Whether you had a whole lot of support from someone else as you mastered the process of riding a bike or you had no support at all and you figured it out all by yourself, the only way you learned was through failing and trying again.

Have you noticed that people who are expert at computer or video games don't read the directions? They learn by failure and keep improving. Once they realize what they did wrong, they adjust quickly.

This is how human beings learn and grow. It's how you learn and grow. It's how the members of your sales team learn and grow, too.

Learning to fail means accepting that failure is part of the human condition. It means recognizing failure's potential as a positive learning experience and not blaming external people or circumstances as a means to cancel it out. It means giving yourself and others the freedom to be more creative, to try new things, to stretch outside your current comfort zone. It means recognizing that, since salespeople are going to fail anyway, you can and should use failure as an opportunity to step back from the blame game and work side-by-side with them. That's the only way you can analyze what went wrong and support them as they figure out how they can do things differently in the future—by letting them fail. Encourage them to analyze their failures to find out what they did right and what they did wrong, and create a plan to deal with those issues in the future.

This dynamic doesn't apply just to salespeople, of course. It applies to everyone, including you. The real you (your identity or self-worth) is perfect, whole, and complete, right now—ten on a scale of zero to ten in terms of your identity and worth as a person. We at Sandler call that sense of inherent, unassailable self-worth "I"-10 for short. Your identity is separate from the role you perform, which can score high or low for any role you choose to assume: manager, parent, poet, cook, you name it. The point is, any role failure is not a verdict on your validity as a person. The real you is and always will be an "I"-10. It's just a question of whether you want to act like and assume your rightful role as an "I"-10. One of the main things "I"-10s do is learn from failure versus externalizing it in the form of the blame game.

Your job as manager is not to reach Never Neverland, that magical place where salespeople finally get over their annoying habit of failing. That world doesn't exist, never did, and never will. Instead, your job is to help them embrace failure and identify with complete clarity the areas within which they are allowed to fail without your disapproval or criticism. Then debrief with them, as an equal, about what happened and what can be learned from it. This discussion is one of the fundamentals of good sales coaching. (See Rule #21.)

A coaching discussion requires an atmosphere of complete trust within the relationship. This is possible through a process called the Three P's of Trust. It's outlined below.

♦ **Potency:** This means setting aside your formal job title and giving the salesperson the right to an opinion, as an equal, within the coaching discussion. It means acknowledging that the salesperson, and not yourself, is in charge of the learning process. It means not pulling rank but being there because you add value.

♦ **Permission:** This means granting the salesperson permission to speak freely and to share all relevant information without fear of judgment. If the salesperson withholds critical information or only shares it cautiously or unwillingly, the discussion may be unproductive. You may end up spending your time dealing with non-threatening surface issues instead of the real problems. You also give your salespeople permission to do what they feel is the best thing to do within their lanes—within the scope of their job duties. Remember salespeople can operate independently within their guidelines.

♦ **Protection:** To help salespeople to feel comfortable speaking freely about failure, the coach must assure them that they are protected from future reprisals for anything said during the private coaching discussion. In other words, no "I told you so," no "gotcha" moments later on where you bring up something the salesperson said in order to win an argument, and no talking behind the salesperson's back. The single exception to protection, of which both parties must be aware, comes when the salesperson admits to unethical or illegal behavior. This has to be dealt with appropriately.

Make the Three P's part of your process. Set the parameters within which your salespeople are allowed to fail, and then debrief privately about what happened when failures occurred. In time, failure will be an accepted part of the culture. You and your team will see it for what it really is: the road to consistent upward growth.

THE SANDLER TAKEAWAY FOR SALES LEADERS

Identify the areas within which it's OK for your salespeople to fail. Then, when they do, debrief without blame about what happened.

1. There is no learning or growth without failure.
2. Make sure you both understand what your lanes are. What are your boundaries?
3. The real you (your identity) is perfect, whole, and complete, right now. Experiencing failure in the roles you perform is not a verdict on your validity as a person.

People Work Harder for Their Reasons Than for Yours

Motivate the individual to hit the corporate goal.

THIS RULE IS all about the neglected art of tying personal goals to corporate goals.

Corporate goals are great. They're important. They need to be there. But on their own, they're not enough. Corporate leaders have to do a little work up front before they can expect people to respond to them.

Corporate goals are typically activity-based, and they focus on commissions and bonuses. Managers say, "OK, here's the deal: If you close X number of deals this quarter, you'll hit your sales goal, and then you'll get a $3,000 bonus." That kind of goal is external in nature. Managers think that will be enough. The truth is, though, it's not. While some people will appear to respond to that kind of goal (because they tied the money in their minds to something they want), it just won't do the job for everyone on your team.

Many leaders will even try to or will ask their managers to motivate the sales team. Since true motivation is from within, however, the familiar corporate motivational strategies and tactics either don't work or (at minimum) don't last. That leaves the members of the company compensation team scratching their heads looking for other ways to motivate the sales team. It's not uncommon for them to hire an outside firm to do variations on the same tactics that already haven't worked. The real solution is much simpler.

What really happens is that people work harder for themselves than they ever will for you. Sometimes it looks like they're working hard for you—but they aren't. Suppose you share that corporate goal built around the $3,000 bonus with one of your salespeople, Sharon, and suppose she goes out and hits it. Here's our question: What really motivated Sharon to do that?

Was there something mystical about the number 3,000? No. Sharon went after that goal for a reason—her reason. You just didn't know what it was. It could have been a desire to be #1 on the team. Or it could have been her lifelong goal to go to Tahiti on the vacation of her dreams. Or maybe Sharon wanted to prove to her mom and dad that she was capable of winning a contest.

The point is: Sharon connected the dots on her own. Not everyone on the staff can be counted on to do that for you. But if you help the members of your team identify what their most important personal goals are and you then tie one of those powerful personal goals to the act of coming to work every day, then they'll motivate themselves. That's the difference between intrinsic (internal/personal) and extrinsic (external/corporate) goals.

The trouble is, most leaders simply aren't in a position to do that because they have absolutely no idea what is important to the people who work for them. They've literally never asked. If you ask ten managers, "Hey, could you give me two goals of people who work for you?," you'd find that only one of the ten, typically, can do it. Most of the time, no one really knows what motivates an individual salesperson. If you don't know who your own people are, you won't know what they want on a more personal and emotional level.

When people like Sharon do seem to get motivated by a corporate goal, what's really happened is that they've done the work for us. They've connected the dots. Most of the people on the team won't do that.

It takes a little work to find out (for instance) that Jim is planning to propose to his fiancée, and he wants to be able to afford to give her a really nice ring. But once you figure that out—what's important to Jim—stand back! He's going to move heaven and earth to hit that goal. Not for you—for himself.

Getting to know your people and figuring out what is most important to them as individuals takes time. It might seem a little awkward and "touchy-feely" at first. But once you move outside your comfort zone and invest that time, you'll realize that this is one of the best investments you can possibly make. Once you help Jim, who hasn't yet connected the dots the way Sharon has, to figure out that he's talking to prospects in order to get that beautiful engagement ring, he'll work a whole lot harder for you. He'll climb mountains you might not have believed it possible that he'd climb.

THE SANDLER TAKEAWAY FOR SALES LEADERS

Take the time to talk to each of your people privately. Use this time to identify a compelling personal goal that really matters to that individual salesperson. Tie the corporate goal to that personal goal. Once you find the right goal, the personal *why*, then you will find that the salesperson is self-motivated.

1. Salespeople who know what they want for themselves work a lot harder than salespeople who just show up for work to keep the boss happy.
2. If you do this for your entire team, you will find that sales productivity goes up dramatically—while staff turnover goes down dramatically.
3. People want work-life balance. Tying work goals to personal goals will help both sides win.

For information on how to get Sandler's Goals Tool, which will help you implement this rule, see the Appendix.

Follow the Four Goldilocks Steps

Use a middle-ground management strategy.

SOME MANAGERS ATTEMPT to manage all aspects of their salespeople's activities. On these teams, whenever salespeople get the sensation that someone is looking over their shoulder, they are usually right—it's the sales manager about to ask for a pipeline report, an opportunity update, a sales forecast, or something else that's heavy on data points.

At the other end of the spectrum are the managers who have a hands-off attitude. They say things like: "I'm only interested in the end result." They may occasionally ask for an update on a specific prospect, but, for the most part, they pay little attention to day-to-day goings-on. Their typical directive to the sales team is, "Just hit your numbers."

Neither management strategy is reliably effective. All too often, in fact, both of these extremes impede productivity.

Too much detail/too little detail. It's a little like the beds in the story of *Goldilocks and the Three Bears*. One is too hard; the other is too soft. There is a middle ground, however, that's just right—a Goldilocks option that keeps your sales team focused on the required day-to-day sales behaviors (and ensures that the long-term results will materialize) without your scrutinizing their every move.

Follow these four steps to pursue an effective middle-ground strategy:

1. **Identify Clear Team Goals.** The first step in helping your sales team members achieve higher levels of productivity is to provide them with clear department goals that connect to a distinct timeline. You can't hold people accountable to specific outcomes unless they clearly understand what it is that they are working toward, specifically what is expected of them, and by when it's expected. People need to see the big picture and understand the part they play in bringing that picture to life. But that's not all they need to see.

2. **Make It Personal.** The next step is to assist your salespeople in translating department goals into individual goals. (See Rule #15.) Those goals should be specific, with clearly defined objectives. A goal to grow a territory by a certain amount between now and 90 days from now, for example, should define how much of that growth should come from existing accounts (and more specifically, which ones) and how much should come from new accounts. The goals should be measurable and time-bound so the degree and rate of progress can be tracked. Finally, of course, they must connect to something that is personally meaningful to each salesperson. (This is a coaching discussion.)

3. **Set Priorities.** Once goals are formulated, they need to be analyzed, organized, and prioritized. High-value goals—those that directly relate to corporate initiatives and contribute to the accomplishment of other goals—should be placed at the top of the list. Ask yourself and the team member: Is there an opportunity to prioritize a goal once considered "top priority" at a lower level?

4. **Collaborate on an Action Plan.** After the goals have been prioritized, you and your team members should co-create individual action plans for accomplishment of the goals. Those plans must be as detailed as the goals themselves. They should include specific steps, taken in a specific sequence, within a specific time-frame, and with specific, measurable outcomes in mind. Rather than focus only on closed sales, focus instead on the trackable activities that precede a closed sale (such as new discussions with unique decision makers).

All four steps are essential, but Step 4 is where the magic starts to happen. The more detailed the plan, the easier it will be for your salespeople to stay on track and measure their progress. If the process derails, a well-defined plan makes the path to getting back on track more visible. It's important that salespeople create the plan. People don't argue with their own data. Once the plan is theirs, they have ownership and commitment to it.

Detailed action plans will provide specific points in time at which you can hold your salespeople accountable for specific actions and outcomes. As a result, you won't have to continually look over their shoulders to see what they're doing—or wait until the end of a quota period to determine what they've done. At key points along their goal-accomplishment journeys, you'll know exactly how far they've come and exactly how much farther they need to go. If a salesperson falls behind schedule, you can provide the needed assistance to help pick up the pace.

Team salespeople with partners who possess complementary skills: the prolific prospector with the adept analyst; the skilled proposal writer with the persuasive presenter. This kind of synergy improves proficiency, productivity, and ultimately profitability. It's "just right."

THE SANDLER TAKEAWAY FOR SALES LEADERS

Sales leaders who commit to the four Goldilocks steps can avoid extremes. They don't need to insist on a single "correct" way of doing things.

1. Be flexible enough to allow team members to flourish in the best environment.
2. Determine what the right approach is for you and your team, and then communicate which approach you are taking so people know what you're doing and how to access you for help.
3. Manage the plan the salesperson puts together and provide coaching and training to help the person achieve the goals.

Only Wear One Hat at a Time

Every sales manager has not one job, but four.

AS A SALES leader, you play different roles during the course of a working day. Your team members may need different kinds of help from you at different times. Your job is to know what the roles are, to be flexible, and to move from one role to another. What's easy to forget is that you can move through different roles in a single conversation with the same salesperson.

This concept of different hats at different times is true at home as well. You have many roles or hats you wear every day. At any given moment you're a spouse, a parent, a chauffeur, a cook, and so on. You have to wear many of these hats. You have to have the ability to move from one to another quickly. You can't say to your family, "Today I am wearing only the spouse hat, and all others issues and needs will have to wait." That wouldn't work. Everyone else would be unhappy.

The same principle holds true at work. When you are leading your people, you have different hats you need to be ready to wear at any given moment. The trick is to be sure you're wearing the right hat at the right time.

The four hats all sales leaders need to be ready to wear are:

- Supervisor
- Trainer
- Mentor
- Coach

The supervisor's job is to monitor performance against specific goals and objectives. Let's say that the salesperson has a commitment to speak, voice-to-voice or virtually, with two C-level decision makers a day. The supervisor's job is going to be to find out whether that actually happened. Supervising should take up about 45% of your time.

The trainer's job is to train salespeople in skills they haven't yet mastered and see that those skills are effectively reinforced over time until they become part of each person's behavior. So if the salesperson in question doesn't yet know how to reach or interact with C-level decision makers, the trainer needs to find a way to help the salesperson learn and reinforce those skills. When you're training, you should be showing the salesperson what to do in a way that makes it easy to follow your example. This should take up about 20–30% of your time, depending on the experience level of your team.

The mentor's job is to be (or create) a success model for the salesperson. So if you yourself are regularly making calls to C-level decision makers and you have a good relationship with the salesperson in question, that salesperson might be motivated to listen in on your calls, look at the emails you send, and use what you're doing to connect with C-level decision makers as a map for his own behavior. What some managers forget, though, is that you can't be a mentor to a salesperson unless there is a healthy, peer-to-peer relationship in place. Mentoring is all about building trust in a given selling model through social interactions. It should take up about 5–10% of your time.

The coach's job is to follow a formal process that uses one-on-one meetings to help salespeople achieve new levels of success by helping them discover hidden issues that inhibit their performance. If the salesperson you're working with has a personal history that makes it difficult to establish initial conversations with C-level contacts, your job is to support the salesperson in figuring out what that obstacle is and how best to overcome it. Contrary to popular belief and practice, effective sales coaching is not "showing them how to do it." Coaching typically accounts for 20–30% of the successful manager's time.

Those, then, are the four hats. Notice that only the first role, the supervisor's role, is based on positional authority. The team member is the salesperson; you're the supervisor. Your job title gives you both the responsibility and the right to check up on whether or not the salesperson is hitting the mark. The both of you may or may not like or respect each other, but it's still your job to check the numbers and make sure the person is doing what they're supposed to be doing.

The other three jobs, however, are based on relationship authority. In other words, if you, the manager, don't have a good one-on-one relationship with the salesperson, you can't do the job in those three areas.

In order to be effective over the long term in each role, you will need to have a process you follow—upon which you constantly improve. The better your process, the more effective you will be at juggling multiple responsibilities.

Specifically, you should have processes for:

* Helping people set goals.
* Motivating your team.
* Hiring and onboarding good people.
* Managing the sales funnel.
* Training your team with the use of role-play.
* Understanding the gaps in your people's skills and designing a plan to improve.
* Coaching.

THE SANDLER TAKEAWAY FOR SALES LEADERS

Sales leaders must be ready, willing, and able to transition between four very different roles—supervisor, trainer, mentor, and coach—all while staying in the Adult ego state.

1. The sales manager's job changes situationally. It's built into the structure of the job so you can't just rely on having strength in only one of these roles. Do the following:
   - Identify what you do in each role.
   - Identify how much time you spend in each role.
   - Identify the most important, highest-impact best practices you can capture in each role.
2. Be flexible. As you talk to different people, be willing to change hats as the situation requires.
3. Remember to create a playbook for yourself.

RULE #18

Create the Curbs on the Roadway

Too much supervision creates learned helplessness.

SUPERVISION, THE FIRST of the four managerial hats from Rule #17, is the manager establishing the behavioral norms and setting up the goals hand-in-hand with the salesperson. It's all about evaluating and sharing feedback on performance in a way that supports salespeople as they grow. It's about monitoring progress and offering suggestions.

Think of the supervisory role as the manager creating the curbs on the roadway. Once that's done, the supervisor and the salesperson can collaborate on the destination toward which the salesperson should drive. The salesperson has the flexibility and the skills to drive toward the chosen destination—but still has the responsibility to avoid running the car up onto the sidewalk.

The supervisor must establish clear behavioral benchmarks with each individual salesperson. Everyone on the team is unique, and everyone needs to be managed individually. This means the supervisor must work with each person to set viable goals, ensure that there is buy-in for the daily mix of behaviors necessary to attain those goals, and also help to formalize the personalized cookbook—the daily action plan for success—that the salesperson will follow. (See Rule #11 for more on the cookbook concept.) Note the emphasis here on customizing the activity plan for each salesperson. Simply announcing that everyone on staff must make 15 cold calls per day isn't effective.

Many sales leaders over-rely on their title—on the supervisory role. I have asked thousands of leaders, as an exercise in Sandler training sessions, to draw a picture of a supervisor. The consistency in the pictures is amazing. There is always someone who is clearly bigger and in charge of someone else. Some even draw in whips! Is this really how to see supervision? If so, this is a problem. A supervisor's authority is exclusively position-based. In other words, your job title is what gives you the potency to issue relevant instructions to the salesperson and to confirm that those instructions are being carried out.

This situation carries both pluses and minuses. On the plus side, salespeople do in fact have to do what you say in order to keep their job. On the minus side, if you over-rely on the supervisory role and under-rely on the other three roles, members of the team may come to think of you as they thought of certain high school teachers who took a bit too much pleasure in holding a position of authority over students. Some managers just look at the CRM or at the emails or reports they receive. The CRM and the digital messages are the only tools they use to manage. They never bother to make salespeople feel valued as individuals, never bother to build up a relationship on a person-to person level. Now ask yourself: Is that how you want the team to think of you?

With that question in mind, please see Rules #19, #20, and #21, which examine the other three roles a sales manager must play during the course of the workday.

THE SANDLER TAKEAWAY FOR SALES LEADERS

Supervision is the manager establishing the behavioral norms and setting up the goals hand-in-hand with the salesperson.

1. Determine how much time you spend with the supervisor hat on.

2. Create a list of activities you perform in the supervisor role.

3. Create guidelines for people to follow and report on.

Train Your Team

Make sure they get the skills they need to do the job.

TRAINING IS THE teaching of new skills. It's where you should be spending 20–30% of your time as a sales leader.

If there's something a salesperson on your team is supposed to be able to do in order to succeed within the position and there's some kind of skill gap that's preventing the person from doing what he's supposed to be able to do, it's your job to make sure the person gets the training he needs to be able to fulfill that requirement. The mistake is training once and thinking the issue is fixed. Some managers even think that training isn't necessary since they have experienced people. Think about your favorite sport to watch or play. Do you think training isn't necessary on an ongoing basis to become better at that sport?

It's worth noting here that your critical responsibility is to make sure the training happens. If you don't want to do the training yourself or you aren't in a position to do so, you can call in someone else. This decision carries with it an important responsibility, however. It is absolutely imperative that you yourself be trained in the same skills that you want your team to be able to execute. You don't have to be as skilled as they are, but your awareness of what they are learning is extremely important.

There are a couple of reasons for this. For one thing, if you don't have and aren't able to use the same skill that the members of the team are supposed to use, you can't possibly role-play that skill in order to help them reach a point of mastery with it. (See Rule #26 for a discussion of the importance of role-play as a tool for turning knowing into owning.)

For another thing, everyone on your team needs to be speaking the same language and using the same system (see Rule #1). That's impossible if your team members have been trained in one system and you're following some other system. Specifically, it's impossible to mentor or coach at full effectiveness if you and the salesperson are using competing systems and tactics.

You will want to conduct a gap analysis for each of your salespeople in order to identify those areas where there's a mismatch between the person's current skill level and the requirements of the job. Once you complete that gap analysis, you will have a good idea of the areas in which each individual needs training and reinforcement over time.

Don't just send people to training and expect everything will be fixed. It doesn't work that way. You can go to a golf school for a couple of days and see lots of things you need to work on. But if you go home and say to yourself, "My game is fixed now," you will be disappointed. Three or four days later, you'll be amazed at how much you forgot and how easy it is to go back to your old ways.

THE SANDLER TAKEAWAY FOR SALES LEADERS

Training, the teaching of new skills, is an important part of the manager's job.

1. It's your job to make sure you know in what areas your people need training—and make sure they receive it.
2. Getting help from an outside training resource is fine. Just make sure you and the salesperson are trained in the same system and are using the same vocabulary in your day-to-day.
3. Have a process for pre- and post-training to make sure what your salespeople learned sticks and is applied.

RULE #20

Mentor to a Success Profile

Create a success model into which people can grow.

MENTORING MEANS PASSING on important thoughts and lessons from one generation to another. Mentoring doesn't have to be based on age, but should be based on expertise.

This isn't training. More often than not, mentoring takes the form of sharing information, talking about specific situations, and getting another perspective by finding out how someone else thinks about circumstances and how that person would approach the situations. Being that "someone else" is an important aspect of the sales leader's job.

There are two schools of thought about mentor relationships on a sales team.

Some people think sales leaders should not try to serve personally in the role of mentor for someone on their staff. The thinking here is that because the manager has formal organizational authority over the salesperson, it's difficult or even impossible to serve as an effective role model when it comes to modeling a given selling behavior in real time—placing a prospecting call to a CEO, for example, or leading a team-selling discussion with an important prospect. There will always be, the people in this school argue, some echo of the manager's position and responsibility resonating around the relationship. Since this echo has the potential to make the transition from knowing to owning more difficult for the salesperson, the manager should (the argument goes) find someone else on the team who can serve as a behavioral role model.

Although I have no problem connecting salespeople with colleagues who can serve as good role models, I do believe that effective sales leaders are capable of playing this role for members of their team. One of the reasons I believe this is that my own most important behavioral role model as a young salesperson was David Sandler, the founder of our company, the creator of the Sandler Selling System—and my boss. My development was dramatic and at a rapid pace. I was a willing participant who came with areas on which I wanted to focus. I was eager to find out how David Sandler thought about certain situations and why he did certain things. To this day I find myself falling back on the lessons and philosophies I learned when we were together. He had a great roadmap for mentorship—perhaps the best roadmap I've ever known. I like to say that David Sandler taught me how to play "sales chess." He taught me the guidelines, how to approach various situations, why certain things were important, and how to think about the right next move. I'm grateful that he was my mentor, and I wish he could have been yours.

If you do opt to take on personal responsibility for fulfilling the mentor role for a salesperson, understand that your success within this role will depend on your ability to create a no-pressure, no-judgment zone in which socialization and reinforcement of skills you've mastered can take place. This should happen while the salesperson watches you execute the skill in question in real time. If you're not comfortable or proficient at this, you should probably pair the salesperson with someone on your staff who has successfully turned the skill into an easy, consistently executed behavior. Typically, this mentor is someone who is already operating at least one level above the mentee.

THE SANDLER TAKEAWAY FOR SALES LEADERS

Mentoring is setting up relationships with people who have strong behaviors in certain main areas that salespeople can use as role models so they can learn to execute those behaviors themselves.

1. If you commit to being a mentor, be sure to have a process. Think about the areas you should focus on, and then create the roadmap to make sure you are adding value.
2. Make a list of people who could mentor the members of your team in different areas.
3. Bear in mind that picking mentors isn't just finding people who can do the job and pairing them with people who can't. You need to match the individuals up with care because the relationship is the key to success.

Empower Your People to Succeed—Without You

Coaching creates wisdom.

GETTING YOUR TEAM to operate on their own and to be self-sufficient is always a critical goal. You should spend 20–30% of your time coaching. Coaching, as we have seen (Rule #17), is one of the four hats a successful manager must be prepared to wear during the course of a working day. It is safe to say this is the least understood of the four roles.

Coaching is all about helping salespeople identify and overcome obstacles to better application of strategies and tactics. It's a series of one-on-one discussions focused on empowering salespeople to apply what they know. To do that, the manager has to be able to focus on the needs of the individual salesperson and to blend them with the needs of the company.

If the relationship the manager has with the salesperson is strong, respectful, and focused on the salesperson's growth as a person, there is the chance for a successful coaching outcome. If the relationship is stressed, marked by unresolved conflict, or lacking in trust, a successful coaching outcome is impossible.

Typically, managers confuse coaching with training, but these are very different activities. When a salesperson comes to the manager's office with a problem, the manager's instant responses may be to try to teach that salesperson something—perhaps by sharing an illuminating personal anecdote and then instructing the salesperson to go forth and do likewise. As the salesperson leaves, the manager thinks, "I am a great coach." Unfortunately, that isn't what coaching is.

Coaching is empowering salespeople to better execute the skills they already have. It is based almost entirely on asking good questions, not on imparting one's own knowledge, opinions, or instructions.

When you're coaching, the big question is not, "What can I tell this person to do?," but, "How do I make a breakthrough based on self-discovery more likely for this person?" (See Rule #22.)

Coaching means setting aside uninterrupted one-on-one time, making sure the salesperson feels safe and comfortable, creating an appropriate up-front contract for the session, and then saying something like, "OK, you remember what we talked about last time: the Sandler concept of pain. I know you understand that. One of the things I'm seeing is that some of the prospects you're working with don't have enough pain to motivate them forward in the sales process. So tell me, how did you go about uncovering pain in your first meeting with ABC Company?" (Salesperson responds.) "And how do you think that went, overall?" (Salesperson responds.) "Looking back on that meeting, do you think there's anything you'd do any differently?"

This is opposed to: "Let me walk you through the sheet with the eight pain questions you were supposed to ask during that meeting—because obviously it didn't stick the last time I gave it to you."

Coaching effectively means leading the salesperson through a process of guided self-discovery. Here is a list of areas you can focus on:

1. **Lead generation:** Prospecting, the #1 behavior that drives all the others.
2. **Building relationships:** Establishing a strong, open relationship based on trust.
3. **Qualifying the opportunity:** Determining a reason to do business.
4. **Making presentations:** Presenting solutions to the prospect's problems.
5. **Servicing customers:** Delivering superior customer satisfaction.
6. **Account management:** Maximizing business in each account.
7. **Territory development:** Building a strategy to grow the territory.
8. **Building a cookbook:** Establishing productive sales activity. (See Rule #11.)
9. **Continuous education:** Developing ongoing product, market, and sales knowledge.
10. **Execution of the Sandler system:** Mastering the sales process.

When talking with a salesperson about one of these areas, you can use the three questions below, in this order, to get a better understanding of where the person needs to focus.

1. "What did you do well in this area?" Or: "What are the things that you're doing right now that are going well?" (The answer might be: "Well, I think I'm pretty good at qualifying prospects.")
2. "What do you think you should be doing more?" Or: "What could you do a little more?" ("I could be asking for more introductions on LinkedIn.")
3. "What do you think you should be doing differently?" ("I think I could be targeting more CEOs in my prospecting outreach.")

Sales coaching is an important and sadly under-discussed topic. To learn more about it, contact your local Sandler trainer—and order our book *The Sales Coach's Playbook*. Use it to create your own coaching playbook.

THE SANDLER TAKEAWAY FOR SALES LEADERS

Coaching is not training.

1. Determine how much time you spend coaching.
2. Coaching is based almost entirely on asking good questions, not on imparting one's own knowledge, opinions, or instructions. Important coaching questions include: "What did you do well?" "What do you think you should be doing more?" "What do you think you should be doing differently?"
3. Create your own coaching playbook.

For information on how to get Sandler's Top Ten Behaviors Tool, which will help you implement this rule, see the Appendix.

People Don't Argue with Their Own Data

Use self-discovery to break through performance barriers.

FUNDAMENTAL SUCCESS COMES from wisdom gained via self-discovery. That's true of selling, as indeed it is true of every other area of human endeavor.

I'm sure you've had this experience: You tell salespeople something from your own experience, something important that you've learned only after a period of major struggle and a whole lot of trial and error. Yet what happens? Very often, the salespeople simply ignore what you've shared. Or, even if they briefly remember what was said, they don't store it or act on it. The lesson here, of course, isn't that what you learned is false or unimportant. It's that salespeople need to self-discover the point that you're trying to share with them. (Or maybe they're just not ready to hear it yet.)

You may already know the answer they need, but you want them to discover that there is a problem and you want them to discover that there is a solution. Once they have discovered the problem for themselves and identified a solution, they are more apt to use that solution. You can tell a salesperson what to do for years and not have it stick. Yet if you ask a powerful question, the kind of question that helps salespeople figure it out for themselves, the pattern can change almost overnight.

There are two big principles to bear in mind about all this:

1. If you tell salespeople something, they tend to deny it. But if they tell you, then it's true!
2. Our experience is that people remember 20% of what you tell them and 90% of what they say and do.

Think about your own life. Have you ever noticed that not many people seem to remember accurately much of what you said but they always seem to remember what they said? It works in the other direction, too, of course. I'm guessing you remember your own words more accurately than other people's.

A good leader takes all this into account and develops an arsenal of good questions. Good questions are your best friends when it comes to supporting a salesperson's self-discovery—but for most of us, the transition from telling what to do to asking good questions is not an easy or intuitive one. It helps to have a list.

Here, then, are two lists of good questions you can practice for your coaching sessions. Use them to help your salespeople create their own wisdom.

Questions about the salesperson's goals and challenges:

◆ "What are you trying to accomplish? What is the goal or problem resolution?"
◆ "What is driving this goal or problem resolution?"
◆ "What actions have you taken so far?"
◆ "What roadblocks do you have to overcome?"

- "What is your level of motivation to change?"
- "What's holding you back from achieving the goal or solving the problem?"
- "What is your level of commitment to success?"
- "How do you benefit from accomplishing the goal or solving the problem?"
- "What meaningful action can you take at this time to make progress?"
- "How can I [the coach] help you achieve the goal or solve the problem?"

Questions about a specific selling opportunity:

- "What was your strategy going in?"
- "What actually happened?"
- "Tell me more."
- "Why do you think that happened?"
- "What tactics did you apply?"
- "What did you do next?"
- "What would you do in this circumstance if you were facing it right now?"
- "Why would you do that?"
- "Suppose you were going to try something slightly different. What would you try?"
- "Is there anything you did you would not have done, knowing what you know now?"
- "What do you think the outcome would have been if you'd done X instead?"

THE SANDLER TAKEAWAY FOR SALES LEADERS

Even though you might want to, you cannot pass your own major hard-won life lessons along to others, not even your salespeople. You can, however, support salespeople as they learn, and you can pose questions that make it easier for them to discover more about themselves and create their own breakthroughs.

1. Ask questions about the salesperson's goals and challenges.
2. Ask questions about specific selling opportunities.
3. Help salespeople discover the issues for themselves. When you say it, they deny it; when they say it, it's true. Your job is to use good questions to get them to verbalize the issue—and then act on it.

RULE #23

Create a Culture of Accountability

Help your people own their success.

A CULTURE OF accountability is the key to a successful team.

Sales leaders like to think of themselves as accountable, but can they honestly say that their sales team operates within a culture of accountability? Since they're leading the team, it's fair to ask that question of the team itself. Do salespeople take ownership? Do they make commitments? Do they live up to their commitments? If the answers are "no," it's fair to ask what needs to change on the leaders' side to fix that situation. Sales leaders must be congruent in mind and action in order for their teams to embrace a culture of accountability.

Here's what often happens. Managers will set agreements and timelines for getting certain things done. They set project deadlines along with all kinds of other benchmarks. They make the commitments themselves, then ask others to make commitments as well. It's all with good intentions. But something happens along the way, and commitments fall through the cracks.

That leads to big problems. For one thing, it's natural for people (managers included) to minimize, or not even be aware, when they themselves have failed to live up to a commitment—and as a result, they don't take responsibility. Second, the victories don't get celebrated. Someone on the sales team accomplishes something, and their manager doesn't even notice.

By the same token, this can sometimes teach salespeople that most of the benchmarks aren't going to be tracked. They can then keep their heads low until the next scurry for benchmarks pops up and this one has been forgotten. They know the manager isn't going to follow up.

These kinds of mistakes breed an atmosphere in which salespeople assume they don't actually have to live up to their commitments and won't be acknowledged even if they do. If you want to create a culture of accountability, a couple of important things have to happen.

First, you need to work on yourself. As the manager, you need to make some public commitments and then make sure you follow through on them—publicly. So your meetings, for instance, should focus more clearly on what is required, when it is required, and who is doing it. As part of that meeting, you, the manager, have to be on point in terms of following through on specific commitments you've made to the team.

Once you make those commitments, you need to stick with them. What you are doing now is called modeling. You're demonstrating by personal example what you want everybody on the team to embody: "My word is my bond."

Can your to-do list still get the better of you? Of course. If you're going to fall short, no problem. Just let everybody know: "I need another 24 hours." (Or whatever time it is you need.) Then deliver on your commitment. The point is, you don't want to step over the commitment or pretend you didn't make it.

Think about your own home life. If you're a parent with teenagers, you know that they are on high alert for signs of inconsistency. When you cut corners, they think, "You're not going to do it; why am I doing it?" That's the dynamic you're dealing with in your sales team. If you want salespeople to have the conviction that they are the company and that their word must be their bond when they are in front of clients, you have to set the example and follow through on it. You have to commit to doing that, not just once in a while, but as a permanent way of doing business. (See also Rule #24.)

THE SANDLER TAKEAWAY FOR SALES LEADERS

Model personal accountability for your team. Be the one who goes there first. Track your own commitments and the commitments of others on the team.

1. You must always keep your word to the members of the team—whether it's on something big or something small. This translates to them keeping their word to the prospect, client, or customer. Be congruent!
2. You can also support a culture of accountability by interacting positively about projects and tasks that are not yet due. (This means you have to track them, of course.) A week or two before the big presentation, you can ask, "Hey, how's the presentation for BigCorp going? Do you need any help?" That tells the person that you are monitoring it and that you are expecting it to be done.
3. Celebrate success. Celebrating success will ensure that your team replicates success.

Share the RACI Stuff

Make sure your people understand roles and responsibilities.

GREAT LEADERS MAKE sure team members know their roles and communicate this to them clearly. That's important because for every project, the people on your team want to know what's going on. They want to know what role they're playing, what they're expected to do, with whom they're working, and what the end result they are working toward is.

A simple, effective model many sales teams use to support accountability in team selling is called RACI. This powerful tool requires you to: a) identify a specific initiative (for instance, a presentation at a major account that will require the work of multiple team members); and b) assign the roles of responsible, accountable, consulted, and informed to particular individuals who are part of that initiative.

Responsible
Accountable
Consulted
Informed

Responsible individuals are those actively involved in implementing and managing the initiative. The list of responsible individuals may extend from salespeople down to the front lines of the organization. People who are responsible for something must know that they are responsible for it—and must know when and how they will be expected to fulfill their responsibility. You, as sales leader, get things done and manage the process.

The **accountable** individual is the one person who is ultimately accountable for the completion of the task and who delegates to those responsible. If the initiative can produce revenue, then you, the manager, may be the one sitting in the accountable box for your sales team. The key point is that there be one and only one accountable person for any project. You may opt to make that person one of your salespeople.

People who are **consulted** are involved in the planning, implementation, and management stages as resources because they possess expertise or have the power to stop or support a project. These individuals could be senior company leaders, members of your board, or trusted advisors on whom you rely for guidance.

Someone who is **informed** doesn't have any involvement other than receiving updates about your project and its progress. Typically, communication with these people is only in one direction, but they're free to weigh in at any time.

Notice again that while there can be lots of responsible people, lots of consulted people, and lots of informed people, one and only one individual can be accountable for the success of a given selling initiative. I emphasize this point because it's imperative that the team knows that when you are in the accountable box, you are choosing to accept personal responsibility for the team's performance, both on the project level and the year-to-date level. If something goes wrong, that's your issue. (On the flip side, if something goes right, be sure to give the credit to the team. Welcome to management, Sandler style.)

Notice, too, that the goal is always to identify specific individual people in all four categories. RACI gives everyone on the team absolute clarity about who's doing what when. It makes it easier for people to stay synchronized on even complex account issues (like who communicates with whom in that big account). It gives your team maximum information, maximum flexibility, and maximum innovation. Use it!

(The RACI matrix is part of Sandler Enterprise Selling, a comprehensive system for selling into complex accounts, which is covered in Rule #31.)

THE SANDLER TAKEAWAY FOR SALES LEADERS

Identify specific individuals designated as responsible, accountable, consulted, and informed for every important initiative that requires cooperation among your team members.

1. Make RACI part of your work process, and accountability will become part of your culture.
2. Pick one person to be accountable.
3. Use the RACI system to identify and engage specific individuals within your organization—do not assign tasks to teams or groups.

For information on how to get Sandler's RACI Tool, which will help you implement this rule, see the Appendix.

RULE #25

Don't Let Your People Leave Training in the Classroom

Create a collaborative, equal partnership inside and outside the training room.

GREAT LEADERS MANAGE the training function of employee development. They make sure the training is working on a skill gap a salesperson has and wants to fill. They set clear goals prior to the program—and they follow up.

Most managers send their people to sales training events with little or no preparation or up-front work. Managers assume that, having guaranteed their salespeople's physical presence in the training room, they can safely check "learning and development" off their to-do list. Convinced that they've fulfilled their responsibility by sending salespeople out for training, they may even feel a little bit of resentment at the time lost. After all, there is no productivity out in the field during the training phase. So they rush people to get back to work. With that choice to rush people into and out of training, managers assume everything is now officially taken care of—at least until the next training session rolls around.

However, when salespeople go back to work, there is frequently no mention of the information learned in the class. The people who went to training are supposed to take something they heard once in a classroom setting and implement it immediately in daily life.

Is that realistic? I don't think so. I don't think you can do it, and I don't think your people can, either. Unfortunately, this common managerial approach pretty much guarantees that the training that just took place isn't going to do anyone any good.

You, the manager, have to commit to certain action items both before and after the training session if you want the training to be effective—which is presumably why you're paying for it. These action items don't have to take a lot of your time, but they do have to happen. They are:

- **Ask questions and set expectations.** Ask the salespeople before they go what they are hoping to learn. Ask things like, "How many good ideas do you think you're going to get out of this training?" Ask, "What do you want to be sure the trainer covers?" Ask, "What do you want to get better at so you are more productive and make more money?" Ask, "What is frustrating you about closing more business?" Listen to the responses you get with both ears.

- **Spotlight at least one important topic before the training takes place.** This assumes that you are synced up with the trainer about what the content of the training is going to be. (That's something Sandler takes very seriously, by the way.) Before the training event, sit down with the salesperson and say something like this: "OK, Keiko—one of the things we talked about during your coaching session was getting through to the decision maker. So that's something I really want you to pay attention to in the training. I'd like you to come out of the session ready to share three things you're going to do differently this week that support that goal of talking to more C-level people." You're really giving Keiko some pinpointed homework before the training session begins.

+ **Debrief on the training after it takes place, and hold the salesperson accountable.** Have a one-on-one coaching session with the salesperson as soon as he gets back. This doesn't have to be a long meeting, but it does have to clarify what the salesperson actually learned, what the homework was (there should always be homework), what specifically the salesperson will be doing to implement what's been learned, and how the learning will be reinforced. Without a shared accountability to implement what's been learned, there will be no sustained behavioral change.

These three action items are just as important as anything that happens inside the training room.

A side note: When my kids were in school, I made sure I knew what they were learning. I wanted to help them understand and practice each new skill. Everyone in the family played an active role in reinforcing the work they did in class. That worked well in our family, and I believe that's the way it should be on sales teams as well.

THE SANDLER TAKEAWAY FOR SALES LEADERS

Invest some time with each salesperson before and after a training event.

1. Ask questions and set expectations (goals) before the training begins.
2. Spotlight at least one important topic for the salesperson to pay attention to during the training. The salesperson should know that you are going to ask about this issue when the training concludes.
3. In a one-on-one session with the salesperson, debrief on the training once it's done. Clarify what was learned, and how it will be put into action going forward.

Role-Play Creates Muscle Memory

The ears have to hear what the mouth is going to say.

PEOPLE LEARN BY doing. Once you do something, you remember it better than you would if you had only read about it or talked about it.

Our experience is that salespeople (and people in general) remember 90% of what they say and do themselves. That means your job as a manager isn't to tell them what to say or do, but to make sure they do it themselves so they can retain it.

Sales leaders don't role-play enough. Frankly, that's malpractice. It's a dereliction of duty. Role-play is a critical component in taking your team's game from knowing to owning. If you do it only rarely (or never), you're letting your team down. It's that simple.

Role-play helps the members of your sales team turn skills they may know about intellectually, but have not yet made habitual, into behaviors they can execute easily and consistently. Role-play is a critical, all-too-easily overlooked tool for growing your team members and supporting them as they move their development to the next stage.

Role-play is what turns theoretical, tentatively applied knowledge into muscle memory.

Everybody has had the experience of changing a tentative or uncertain way of executing an important task into muscle memory. It's about practicing something until it becomes second nature. Can I assume that you've got a driver's license and that you're comfortable driving home from work at the end of the day through heavy traffic while listening to the radio? If so, that means driving a car, which was once something you didn't know how to do at all and was then something you did only tentatively, is now muscle memory. It has become second nature.

When you send your team members out on a sales call for which you depend on them executing skills they have not yet turned into muscle memory, you are sending them out on the highway to navigate high-speed traffic for the first time—without a learner's permit! Role-play with them to teach them the rules of the road.

The first step of a good role-play session is for you to make it clear which specific skill or area of the sales discussion you're hoping to help the salesperson (or the group watching) to master. For instance, opening the meeting with a strong up-front contract. Don't try to role-play the entire call—it's too long.

The second step is for you as the leader to play the salesperson. The salesperson gets to play prospect or customer. Why is that important? Adults learn by imitation and illustrations. They tend to want to watch and model. When your team members can model what they've seen you do, it's easier for them to learn. What doesn't work is to say to your team, "OK, let's role-play this. I want each of you to show me how you would open the meeting." They don't know how to do it yet at the level of mastery—or may not know how to do it at all—so they will feel uncomfortable. If you don't play the salesperson's role first, you will put the members of the team into in a not-OK scenario.

The third step is to make sure the salesperson owns it. Right now it's your script, your approach. You need the salesperson to own it so ask: "What would you change?" Ask: "How did you feel about that?" Follow up with questions like: "If you were the customer, how would you react to what just happened?" And: "If it were up to you, what would you change about the role-play we just did?" Allow the salesperson to change it. Do the role-play again, if necessary, on the salesperson's terms.

The fourth and final step is to give your salespeople something to practice and to let them practice it with you first. This should be the takeaway from the role-play you just completed. For instance, help your salespeople practice the specific wording of the up-front contract they are going to propose at their next meeting.

Once you've done all that, congratulate yourself. You've used role-play to support the salesperson—and the team. Now, determine your top ten role-play scenarios and create a cookbook for them. What has to happen every time in order for them to be successful? Write it all down.

THE SANDLER TAKEAWAY FOR SALES LEADERS

Use role-play to support salespeople in the transition from tentative execution of a skill to muscle memory.

1. The more you role-play, the better you get.
2. Determine your top ten role-play scenarios.
3. Create a cookbook for your top ten role-play scenarios.

Sweeping Issues under the Carpet Only Ruins the Floor

Your credibility with others on the team is determined by how you handle tough issues.

REMEMBER THOSE MONKEYS? "See no evil, hear no evil, speak no evil." It's an interesting image, but unfortunately, following the monkeys' example by covering your ears and eyes doesn't make a problem go away. (Actually, "speak no evil" is probably a pretty good idea, but I digress.)

Turning a blind eye or a deaf ear isn't the way to manage a team. As a leader, you are held to a high standard. You have to deal with issues just as you would want your salespeople to deal with them with buyers. Congruency is key.

When we ask sales leaders how they deal with the inevitable problems, conflicts, and misunderstandings that arise on the sales team, many appeal to something called the "72-hour rule." Maybe you've heard of this rule. The basic principle is to wait 72 hours and see if the problem goes away on its own. (What is more likely is that the issue doesn't go away at all; people just get tired of waiting for you to act.)

This is not a great approach to conflict management—or any other tough interpersonal issue, for that matter. Let's face it: The "wait awhile to see if it disappears" rule frustrates and stresses salespeople. When they have a problem with a colleague and it's obvious that management knows about the problem and is choosing to do nothing about it, some salespeople will indeed go silent. That means that after 72 hours (or more), the manager will conclude that the problem has gone away. But in fact it hasn't. It's gotten worse. Now one of the combatants has an internal monologue that sounds like this: "Wow—they're going to let that stand. I guess the inmates are running the asylum around here. I'd better look for somewhere else to work."

A better approach is to bring the parties together in private and say, "I could tell there was a disagreement this morning. I know there seems to be a problem here, and I want to get to the bottom of it and find out what the best way to fix it is. What do you think happened?" Then let both sides have their say, ask good questions, listen to the answers, and make a decision. That's one of the things leaders get paid to do: make decisions. So do that. Be courageous five minutes at a time. You only have to have enough courage to start the process.

Despite what you may have been told or been led to assume, the 72-hour rule is a recipe for a dysfunctional sales team. It's sweeping a messy problem under the carpet—but that only ruins the floor.

Think of this kind of problem solving in the same way an outside consultant would. A good consultant will tell you that, in reality, the faster you deal with a problem, the easier it is going to be to deal with that problem. If you let Salesperson A get away with something for two months and then finally sit him down and say, "You've got to stop doing that," what's going to happen? Salesperson A is going to jump right into the victim corner of the Drama Triangle (see Rule #7). He's going to say, "Wait a minute—I've been doing that for a long time now, and so has Salesperson B and Salesperson C." Salesperson A will be right about that. When you press the point, everybody's going to be demotivated.

The moral is simple: Take action sooner rather than later when you know there's a problem on the team.

THE SANDLER TAKEAWAY FOR SALES LEADERS

When you spot a problem, call a private meeting right away, even if you aren't looking forward to the discussion.

1. Bring the participants together. Find out what's really happening and try to work out the best way forward—together.

2. Ask good questions and listen to the answers. (For instance: "How would doing X in such-and-such a way affect you, Salesperson A? What would the potential downside be?") See if the participants can solve the issue with a little open-ended questioning from you. For instance: "Salesperson B, what is a way forward that everyone can live with?"

3. When you've heard everyone out, make a decision. That's your job as leader.

RULE #28

A Sales Meeting Is Your Sales Presentation

Master the skills that support a great sales meeting.

WE'VE ALREADY SEEN (in Rule #10) that the job interview is to the sales manager what the initial sales call is to the salesperson. Here's another parallel to consider: Any time you conduct a sales meeting with the team or one of its members, that's the equivalent of the salesperson's presentation to a prospect or customer. That's fulfillment: You share information and get a clear commitment to move forward together on a common objective.

A big part of your responsibility as sales manager is to help your sales team to increase their own capacity to perform and improve the outcomes of their performance—in other words, to help them help themselves become better salespeople. To that end, conduct regular sales meetings to clarify shared goals and support accountability, provide one-on-one coaching to keep individual salespeople on track, and deliver training when needed.

What can you do to improve the outcomes of your performance when you're conducting those sales meetings, providing the coaching, and delivering the training? What can you do to improve your closing ratio on shared commitments? The short answer is: plan.

It is the manager's job to do the necessary work for the sales meeting up front. That means that, before the meeting begins, you must:

* Figure out what kind of meeting you need to hold. Are you providing information? Discussing unresolved issues? Planning strategies/actions? Solving problems? Managing crises? Reporting performance? Establishing targets and objectives? Identifying tasks and delegating responsibilities? Some combination of two or more of these things? Establish the purpose and objectives of this specific meeting. Don't assume that the same necessity that drove your last meeting should drive this one.

* Identify the agenda items. Obviously, this agenda should support the purpose(s) you identify. Create a written agenda. Share it with attendees.

* Identify required attendees. If certain people don't need to be at this meeting, don't require their attendance.

* Identify all the resources and support materials that will be needed. Work this out ahead of time.

* Determine time requirements. Know about how long the meeting is going to take.

* Create, ahead of time, an up-front contract that supports all of the above. If you don't know what the up-front contract is going to be, there's no way you can set it with the team.

* Conduct the meeting. You must serve as the facilitator. That means you must:

  ◇ Set and defend the up-front contract for the meeting. It's hard to overstate how important this is. The degree of ease and comfort you show in setting this contract at the beginning of the meeting and defending it as the meeting moves forward will have a direct impact on your team's skill when it comes to setting up-front contracts with their prospects.

◇ Encourage interaction. Find a way to get everyone involved.

◇ Facilitate discussion. Make sure people feel safe expressing their opinions.

◇ Stick to the agenda. (See Rule #29.)

◇ Stick to the time allotted. Watch your time investments.

◇ Promote agreement; resolve conflicts. Praise team members who put personal interests and concerns aside in support of the team. Be a fair arbiter of disputes.

◇ Summarize key points. Know when enough discussion is enough. Step in and isolate the main ideas, and then move on.

◇ Identify and assign action steps. Use the RACI system. (See Rule #24.)

◇ Establish a time, date, and place for the next meeting. Just as with a sales call, you want to establish the next step before you close the meeting.

◆ Follow up. The decisions and action steps arising out of the meeting need to be honored, and as the manager, you must take the lead in making sure that happens. That means you should:

◇ Formalize the notes. Take the time to create a written summary of what just happened. If you need help with this step, get it.

◇ Make sure the notes are distributed after the meeting. Email makes this easy.

◇ Confirm agreed-upon actions and responsibilities. Follow through on the RACI commitments. Remind people about who's doing what. Don't wait until the last minute.

◇ Conduct a fearless self-inventory of your outcomes as the leader of the meeting. There's always something you could have done better. Find out what it is.

THE SANDLER TAKEAWAY FOR SALES LEADERS

When you take part in a sales meeting with the team or with an individual, that's the equivalent of the salesperson's presentation. You are either going to get a meaningful, reliable commitment to move forward on a shared objective—or you aren't.

1. Prepare for a meeting the way you want your salespeople to prepare for a call.
2. Determine what type of meeting you need; prepare an outline and agenda to share with others; set and defend an up-front contract that supports that agenda; and follow up after the meeting.
3. Conduct a fearless self-inventory of your outcomes.

Don't Chase Purple Squirrels

Stay focused and stick to the agenda during sales meetings.

IF YOU'RE NOT careful, you can spend a whole lot of time during sales meetings talking about topics that you weren't supposed to be talking about.

Some salespeople specialize in raising these kinds of topics. They may have many reasons for doing so. Maybe they're bored. More than likely, though, it's because they'd rather talk about something else than what's on the agenda. Often, they start asking you questions like, "Hey, do you remember how, last February, we were going to [insert old issue here]? Whatever happened to that?"

That's a purple squirrel (also known as a red herring). It's comparable to the weird (or maybe imaginary) animal your dog sees, but you don't, while you're out on a walk. Suddenly you find yourself being pulled in a direction you didn't want to go.

A classic purple squirrel is an in-depth discussion about an (alleged) sales opportunity brought to you as a starting point of a new business relationship. Salespeople may present the pursuit of this opportunity as a viable "foot in the door" strategy and may try to consume a great deal of the team's time discussing it (as opposed to, say, the overall state of their pipeline.) Typically, though, the buyer isn't considering giving your company much business. They may simply be looking for someone to do something none of their partners want to do.

You try to take a buyer's business pain and create a solution—which is great—but before you invest a lot of the team's time discussing this opportunity, bear in mind that if you are chasing deals that aren't in your strike zone, then it's a lot of time, work, and effort with a high probability of the deal going sideways. In other words, this should probably be a two-minute time investment during the sales meeting, not fifteen. (Yes, you do want to invest those two minutes because you want to make sure none of the deals in the pipeline are purple squirrels.) There is some evidence to suggest that the length of salespeople's bloviating is in direct correlation to how eager they are for you not to notice how poorly they are doing. Don't fall for it.

Or let's say you're beginning a discussion about the sales funnel—who's got what opportunities, how many opportunities are actually in the funnel at its various stages, and what's happening next in each case—and one of the salespeople leans in before you can get started and says, "Just out of curiosity—what are we doing about the compensation program? Wasn't there supposed to be a memo about that last week?"

If you let the sales funnel discussion degenerate into a purple squirrel discussion about the compensation plan, you have lost control of the topic and the meeting. That question about the memo you were all supposed to get may or may not be a legitimate topic—but it's not the one you are there to talk about. By the way, this is one of the big reasons you need a good agenda and a good up-front contract before a sales meeting—or any meeting. It needs to be clear to everyone in the room what the ground rules of the meeting are going to be, what's on the list of discussion points, and what's not.

How do you handle a purple squirrel when it comes up? Very quickly! Right away, say something along the lines of, "Alex, you know, that's a great topic—but not for today. Let's handle that one offline." Then, after the sales meeting, connect with Alex and deal with his issue with full attention and respect.

There are two big reasons purple squirrels materialize during meetings. One is that salespeople aren't prepared and they're hoping to change the subject. (Don't let them.) The other is that they have a question they feel they're not going to get answered unless they pose it publicly. (Answer it for them—just not at the expense of your sales meeting's agenda.)

THE SANDLER TAKEAWAY FOR SALES LEADERS

If a salesperson goes off topic during a sales meeting, redirect quickly.

1. Be aware that changing the subject during a sales meeting may be a sign that the salesperson is throwing purple squirrels.
2. It's also possible that salespeople can have questions that they don't feel will be addressed unless they're asked publicly. Meet offline with them and resolve the issue.
3. Make sure deals in the funnel aren't purple squirrels.

KARE for Your Customer

Create strategies that match your target.

KARE PROFILING IS a powerful strategy component in territory management that tags each of your prospects and clients with one of four designations:

- "K" for current clients you want to **keep**.
- "A" for accounts you don't have, but wish you could **attain**.
- "R" for customers you used to have and now would like to **recapture**.
- "E" for current accounts where you wish your "wallet share" could **expand**.

The beauty of this system lies in its simplicity. The four categories you just read can be complemented by any criteria you decide are relevant to the team and the market you serve—but the core idea behind each corner of the quadrant is absolutely impossible to misunderstand. There are really only two principles to follow here:

1. Every "live" opportunity with whom you actually want to work has to go somewhere on this KARE model.

2. No opportunity can occupy two slots of the KARE quadrant. You have to pick one.

These designations allow you and your team to segment and prioritize your targets. They also provide a base of understanding and clarity in team-selling environments.

The KARE process also provides an invaluable sales management tool. Once you've identified the accounts that fit in each quadrant, you can identity the strategies you will implement in each of the quadrants.

Below, you will find some of the most common attributes arising from a KARE profiling session. Of course, the actual attributes relevant to your market must arise from your own evaluation of your organization's business model.

Keep	Attain
Current maintenance client Acceptable profitability Minimal growth potential Low level of vulnerability Acceptable relationships Minimal investment Managed service costs	New business target Profile match Low level of vulnerability Projected acceptable profitability Projected acceptable growth potential Acceptable pursuit investment Neutral relationships
KARE	
Recapture	**Expand**
Inactive previous client Low level of vulnerability Variable growth potential Acceptable profitability Variable relationships Variable pursuit investment	Current major client High profitability Strong growth potential High level of vulnerability Significant relationships Investment target for growth

If you wish, your teams or territories can be structured using KARE as a base. One strategy might be to focus certain salespeople on particular profiles—for instance, with one group focused on A (Attain) accounts, and another on E (Expand) accounts. Alternatively, the focus might be to blend into each team or territory a mix of all profiles, in order to keep salespeople and teams nimble and capable of serving all profiles.

Your people should have a cookbook that lays out how much time and what kind of activity will be spent in each quadrant. This way you will have a well-rounded, focused approach.

You want to make conscious choices here. Following the path of least resistance is not in anyone's best interest. The worst outcome is to have your people focusing 100% of their attention on, say, Keep—and nothing at all on Attain, Recapture, or Expand. Identify a target percentage of time for each salesperson to spend on each activity.

THE SANDLER TAKEAWAY FOR SALES LEADERS

The KARE Account Planning Tool empowers your sales process by delivering value in territory and account planning.

1. Utilize the profiling tool for both current clients and prospects that creates a common organizational lexicon through four simple categories: Keep, Attain, Recapture, and Expand.
2. KARE facilitates a more comprehensive account understanding on the part of everyone on the team—including you.
3. Identify opportunities within each quadrant; develop strategies for each quadrant; and set targets for how much time you want your team to focus on each area.

Your Best Prospects Are Your Current Customers

Focus on the complete sales cycle; create a plan—and an environment—that allows you to do much more business with each other.

THIS CHAPTER IS all about two questions that most sales managers encounter at one point or another in their careers:

1. What is enterprise selling?
2. Are the skills and approach the same as in more familiar sales cycles?

Also known as "major account " or "complex account" selling, enterprise selling means selling into organizations that present one or more of the following challenges to the selling team: extended sales cycles; sophisticated competition; significant financial investment in pursuits; cross-functional teams; a focus on long-term business value rather than short-term pricing; wide, diverse buyer networks; complex decision structures; and/or a highly diversified organization and footprint.

Enterprise selling is to traditional sales as chess is to checkers. It carries potentially huge rewards for the sales organization and its team members—but it also carries immense risks that must be managed intelligently.

For years, sales managers asked us: "How do we win business with large enterprise organizations, serve them effectively, and expand the relationship over time?" Those business objectives sound simple enough, but we at Sandler quickly realized that they presented unique opportunities and unique challenges.

To begin with, enterprise sales cycles have the kinds of complex, shifting timelines and ongoing logistical challenges that other types of selling simply don't need to address. Not only that—buyer networks within these companies are far more complicated than in other types of selling, presenting a much wider array of agendas and organizational functions within the decision tree than networks at smaller companies.

These buyers are demanding. Enterprise clients expect deep preparation and a thorough understanding of their business. While research is critical, just doing the right research is nowhere near enough. You must position your solutions and offerings properly, based on an informed assessment of the client's business, market, culture, and customer base. Having a clear picture of those key elements allows you to align your product/service to the needs of the client organization and all of its relevant stakeholders.

The kind of alignment that wins enterprise clients has its roots in the delivery of strategically important business value. This alignment is not rooted in discussions of features or benefits, but in clearly demonstrating compelling value that is uniquely connected to specific client needs through a strong business case.

Competitively pursuing enterprise accounts—to say nothing of winning, growing, and retaining them—represents a significant investment of the selling company's human, financial, management, and logistical resources. In order to justify those investments, multiple parts of the selling organization must work together. The business value of the proposed solutions you identify, develop, and implement must be absolutely unassailable—because the competition you will face is likely to be both sophisticated and relentless.

This kind of selling process, in short, demands the very best from each and every member of the selling organization who takes part in its execution. To meet this challenge, Sandler launched Sandler Enterprise Selling (SES) in 2014, based on the Sandler Selling System methodology created by David Sandler. The SES program and tools provide a practical approach for increasing sales effectiveness in serving enterprise organizations. They don't replace the familiar Sandler principles, but augment and expand them so that they can be applied in the enterprise world.

Take the time to figure out whether it makes sense for you and your team to compete in this challenging, demanding, rewarding arena. If it does, you will want to become familiar with the six stages of the SES program. These are represented in the following graphic.

1. **Territory & Account Planning:** Setting a strong baseline for success through comprehensive planning.
2. **Opportunity Identification:** Analyzing, assessing, and initiating interaction on the opportunities with the highest probability of victory.
3. **Qualification:** Executing a practical plan to engage with the enterprise buyers, who will clarify the key parameters of the opportunity and improve and reinforce your position.
4. **Solution Development:** Crafting a compelling, team-developed solution that directly addresses the specific needs and pains of the enterprise organization and the most influential individuals within it.
5. **Proposing & Advancement:** Finalizing and delivering the client-focused solution and acting on the resulting decision to achieve advancement.
6. **Service Delivery:** With the business relationship active, coordinating team activities to maximize client satisfaction and grow the account.

Mastery of all six of these stages and use of the proprietary tools contained within each is essential if your aim is to win and retain enterprise clients.

SES, which has been field-tested extensively, does not require any familiarity with the core Sandler principles. It will come as no surprise, though, to learn that this program is rooted in David Sandler's fundamental selling philosophies—and in his (and our) best practices, honed over a period of decades.

THE SANDLER TAKEAWAY FOR SALES LEADERS

Enterprise selling is to traditional selling as chess is to checkers.

1. The Sandler Enterprise Selling program offers a proven system for winning and retaining enterprise clients.
2. SES augments and expands familiar Sandler Selling System principles.
3. Its six stages are Territory & Account Planning, Opportunity Identification, Qualification, Solution Development, Proposing & Advancement, and Service Delivery.

Use Brainstorming to Maximize Bandwidth

Group brainstorming captures the best ideas and makes them easier to implement.

RAPID GROUP BRAINSTORMING is an essential component of managing effective sales teams. You must have, and use, a process that brings together all the client-serving resources in your organization, and you must be able to work together to resolve problems and act on opportunities. In other words, you must know when and how to generate a storm of ideas.

There's a tool for sales teams that does exactly this. It's called Team Storm. People want to be heard and to contribute their ideas. When your team members have the opportunity to share and participate, they are more likely to see the project through. A "we" idea has a much better chance of success than a "me" idea.

The Team Storm process provides an effective vehicle for driving rapid, real-time collaboration on behalf of an emerging opportunity or a pressing client/customer issue. It is recommended for use in situations where there are urgent, time-sensitive problems to resolve, and also for those situations where you are simply trying to deliver the best possible service in a timely manner to prospects or customers. It is especially effective when the challenge is getting the service and delivery teams and sales and account management teams to work in harmony with one another.

Team Storm is a rapid, structured, group decision-making tool that brings together contributors from all areas of the organization. It's a highly participative team-building event that dares people to put down the phones and turn off the computer for 20–30 consecutive minutes. You read right. This is a low-tech, high-touch session using flip-charts and markers. The reason to keep it low-tech is that the low-tech approach actually engages people. Try it—it works.

When should you use Team Storm?

- When you have a group problem to solve.
- When you need fast action and practical results for a prospect or customer.
- When you have access to people with the background, interest, and motivation to solve the problem.
- When you need full accountability.

The Team Storm process has five steps:

1. **Problem statement:** The facilitator shares a concise, accessible summary of the opportunity, problem, or challenge, writing it prominently and legibly on the flip-chart or whiteboard. This writing must remain visible throughout the session. Possible session objectives include:

   - How to serve Client/Prospect X more effectively.
   - How to take advantage of a specific new opportunity to serve Client/Prospect X.
   - How to anticipate the future needs of Client/Prospect X.

- How to identify the actions needed to ensure a multiyear (five-plus) relationship with Client/Prospect X.
- How to communicate more effectively as a team in serving Client/Prospect X.
- How to identify specific actions that will increase Client/Prospect X's satisfaction.

2. **Background:** The facilitator leads a discussion about any additional information, clarification, or constraints the team as a whole needs to know about. This is important because not all work groups will share the same level of familiarity with the opportunity or challenge being examined. The facilitator should also set ground rules, making it clear that this is not the time for questioning as to how or why.

3. **Idea generation:** The facilitator begins and supports an active, engaged, creative thinking session, helping the team to generate as many ideas in as short a time span as possible and ensuring that all ideas are recorded on the flip-chart or whiteboard. During this phase of the discussion, the emphasis is on quantity over quality. The facilitator should assume, and help everyone else assume, that for the purposes of this meeting, there is no such thing as a bad idea. This is the brainstorming portion of the program.

4. **Idea selection:** The facilitator leads the discussion in which the team as a whole reviews the final idea list. The facilitator oversees a voting process that identifies the top four ideas.

5. **Action plan/next step:** The facilitator leads the discussion through which the team's top choices become action items. Who will do what? When? Be specific. Focus on individuals and clear timelines, not groups and unquantifiable goals. (This phase of the Team Storm process can benefit from the use of the RACI accountability matrix, which is discussed in Rule #24.)

This process may not solve every problem you encounter as a sales manager, but it is a remarkably effective tool for identifying new approaches to problems or challenges that could have a negative impact on relationships with clients and prospects. The keys to its success are speed and engagement.

Here's a handout that helps keep facilitators and team members on track during the rapid-fire Team Storm process. Use it.

Team Storm Tool

FACILITATOR ROLE	TEAM MEMBER ROLE
The Team Storm facilitator leads the discussion, driving the key activities. These include: • Directing the process • Clarifying, summarizing and developing the team's ideas • Motivating and assisting • Keeping the team focused	The other members of the team work to develop a solution and develop actions by: • Sharing ideas • Sharing suggestions • Sharing builds • Maintaining a supportive, team-focused attitude of listening and encouraging

Remember that Team Storm is a group exercise that must be led by a facilitator. This tool is not meant to be used by a single person.

The facilitator should use a flip-chart or whiteboard to work through each of the Team Storm steps with the team. The blanks below can be used to record the key elements resulting from this session. Assign one person to take down the most important points.

 Step 1: Problem Statement
(What is the concise version of the opportunity, challenge or problem?)

 Step 2: Background
(What additional information, clarification or constraints should the team know?)

 Step 3: Idea Generation
(Active engagement; creative thinking; quantity over quality.)

 Step 4: Idea Selection
(Team reviews final idea list; votes for top four most likely to lead to solution.)

 Step 5: Action Plan/Next Steps
(Top choices become actions. Who does what, when?)

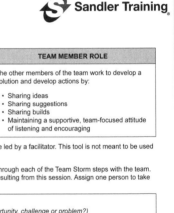

THE SANDLER TAKEAWAY FOR SALES LEADERS

The Team Storm process can help you harness the power of group brainstorming to create innovative solutions on behalf of your prospects and customers.

1. The facilitator leads the session.
2. Teammates work to build a solution and develop actions by sharing ideas, suggestions, and extensions of each other's concepts.
3. The Team Storm session can't solve every problem, but it can create remarkable new approaches, especially on issues that involve both service delivery and sales teams.

Live the Success Triangle

Use the proven formula for sales success.

MOST SALESPEOPLE THINK of success in terms of accomplishments, like winning a major account, reaching sales goals, earning commission bonuses, winning sales awards, or getting promoted.

All of these achievements are signs of success, the result of the convergence of three core elements:

+ Behavior—muscle memory, what a person actually does (see Rule #26)
+ Attitude—belief, outlook, and expectations
+ Technique—strategies and tactics

To more fully understand the concept of "success," think of it as a triangle with each core element—attitude, behavior, and technique—representing one point. Each point is connected to the other two, and it is those connections that provide strength to the structure.

Confidence
Outlook
Responsibility

ATTITUDE

SUCCESS

TECHNIQUE

BEHAVIOR

Goals
Plans
Actions

Strategy
Preparation
Focus

We call this the Success Triangle. Good techniques and behaviors, on their own, aren't enough to generate substantive, lasting success. If the attitude element of the Success Triangle goes unaddressed, achievements are superficial and unreliable, without the personal aspect that gives meaning and color to accomplishments. Similarly, a great attitude and mastery of technique don't add up to anything if there is no consistent behavior in support of the goal. There is an interconnectedness to the three elements.

We teach the success formula this way to reinforce a critical point, one that can't be overemphasized: It's impossible to reach high levels of success with only one or two of these three elements in place. You need all three. This is true for you as a manager, and it is equally true for each and every one of the salespeople who report to you.

If you are going to reach the highest levels of personal and professional success, you must work on all three of these elements and so must the members of your team. You must create positive affirmations. You must create a cookbook. You must identify the top ten things at which you want to be great.

The unique challenge managers face lies in finding the emotional switch that triggers an individual salesperson's passion to succeed, activates appropriate growth and confidence in all three corners of the triangle, and translates the salesperson's passion into goals and plans of action that are focused on and benefit the business.

This is the ongoing mission of a great sales leader—and in a sense, it's a goal that can never be marked off as completed. It's really the ongoing work of a lifetime, both for yourself and for the members of the team. It's rooted in a deep understanding of how all three points of the Success Triangle work.

In the chapters that follow, we will look in depth at each distinct element of the Sandler Success Triangle.

THE SANDLER TAKEAWAY FOR SALES LEADERS

Attitude, behavior, and technique are the three points on the Sandler Success Triangle. You and the members of your team need all three.

1. How important is having a positive attitude? Very important. Yet many people don't realize that, on its own, a positive attitude accomplishes little or nothing if it isn't channeled into an effectively executed plan.

2. Similarly, even the best behaviors are doomed to fail if they are not backed by a supportive attitude and implemented with the requisite skills. Create a cookbook.

3. A solid technique, on its own, won't accomplish much unless it's applied to an appropriate framework of behavior with a positive expectation of success. Identify the top ten things at which you want to be great.

Harness the Power of Behavior

Use the power cycle of goals, plans, actions, and accountability.

CONSIDER YOURSELF A scientist. Understand exactly what it takes for you to meet your goals, and also what it takes for the members of your team to meet theirs.

Bear in mind that behavior controls attitude. You can change your attitude by doing the behavior. You may not feel like exercising at 5:30 in the morning—but when you suit up and start jogging, you're going to find that your head follows along. The Sandler Success Triangle you saw in Rule #33 really is the roadmap to success. To get the most out of a roadmap, you have to have a starting point. Whenever you are using this roadmap, you have to make sure your salespeople begin with behavior—with muscle memory, with action.

Understand that behavior—what you actually do repeatedly, what becomes second nature—is the starting point on the journey to success. David Sandler used to say: "Do the behaviors! Do the behaviors! Do the behaviors!" He emphasized the point because he knew that taking consistent action on a properly trained and reinforced skill is the very best way to generate positive momentum. He wanted salespeople to begin their journey to success with the powerful cycle of goals, plans, and actions.

That's why it is so important to do the gap analysis mentioned in Rule #19. That analysis allowed you to figure out which behaviors each of your individual team members can already do well and can execute from muscle memory—and which areas still need to be trained or reinforced. Begin, if you can, with the salesperson's existing strong suit. Lead with action. Build up that muscle memory.

Some managers feel they need to start with attitude, with changing the person's belief system. We disagree. Start with behavior. If you try to lead with attitude, with getting the salesperson's belief system "straightened out," there will be problems. Put the belief question on hold and help your salespeople get into the position where they can simply do the right behaviors, day after day.

In Rule #21, I shared with you the top ten behaviors for field salespeople. Please go look at them again. If for some reason, you haven't yet conducted a gap analysis for each individual salesperson on your staff in each of these areas, do so right now. If something on that list has been learned by one of your people but hasn't yet been made part of a repetitive behavior pattern, part of muscle memory, then it's not yet a behavior—it's a skill. Figure out what's already in place and what skills need improvement.

The behaviors that salespeople must perform—in all ten areas—must be turned into goals, and those goals must have the unconditional commitment from the salespeople for achievement. Once the goals are set, the manager's job is to help salespeople create a strategy to achieve the goals—as well as confirm the action steps that are necessary to execute the goals. If you do that and get your salespeople to take action, the beliefs will catch up to the behaviors as their confidence and proficiency grows.

Let me emphasize that your team members must each create a personal cookbook and follow it daily. (See Rule #11.) A cookbook must be a living document; it needs to be adjusted constantly. Once a viable cookbook is established and is being followed on a daily basis, you can provide training and coaching to help the members of your team succeed. Don't forget that you, as the leader, need a cookbook, too.

There are a few fundamental core beliefs that do need to be in place—discussed in Rule #35—and these should probably be considered when you are establishing your hiring criteria. The general principle for getting started on the journey to success, though, remains the same one David Sandler shared decades ago and that we continue to repeat today: Do the behaviors, do the behaviors, do the behaviors!

THE SANDLER TAKEAWAY FOR SALES LEADERS

Do a gap analysis. Figure out which behaviors each one of your individual team members is already strong in and can execute from muscle memory—and which areas still need to be trained or reinforced.

1. Fill in the gaps and help the salesperson leverage the cycle of goals, plans, and actions. That means doing the right behaviors, over and over, day after day.

2. Some managers feel they need to start with attitude, with changing the person's belief system. Sandler disagrees. Start with behavior. If you lead with behavior, with muscle memory, the beliefs will catch up.

3. Make sure your team members have their own cookbooks, and create a cookbook for yourself.

Attitude Matters

Success is located between the ears—so master the three core beliefs all successful salespeople share.

ATTITUDE, THE SECOND point on the Success Triangle, is simply belief. For people to achieve their full potential, their belief system should support their behavior plan and vice versa. As you saw in Rule #34, Sandler believes that salespeople's belief systems can catch up to their vigorously executed behavioral plan because from the behaviors they will gain confidence in their abilities.

It is fair to ask, though: What is the least the person needs to have in terms of belief? What kind of belief system should you, the manager, be looking for at the very beginning of your relationship with someone applying for the position of salesperson?

First and foremost, salespeople need to have a strong belief in themselves. They should have that before they even get started with your team. David Sandler used to say, "We perform in a manner that is consistent with how we see ourselves conceptually"—a quote we would like to have memorized and repeated out loud daily by every sales manager responsible for interviewing to fill an open slot on any team. How do applicants see themselves conceptually? How do you know? Are job applicants, for instance, seeking your personal validation—trying to get emotional needs for approval met during the interview? If so, that's not a good sign for their ability to interact on a peer-to-peer basis with prospects. Are the applicants' concepts of self-worth strong?

In addition, the manager has to make sure there is the potential for a strong belief in the company. People who have doubt in the company can't go out there and compete. This potential can be confirmed during the interview process and strengthened during onboarding. Of course, it should go without saying that your own level of belief in the company will affect that of the people on your team.

Finally, the manager has to make sure that the salesperson has a strong belief in the potential of the marketplace. The salesperson has to believe the marketplace is one of abundance, not scarcity. This, too, is something you can learn to pick up on during the interview process.

Remember:

- You want your people to have confidence and conviction in themselves and the company. You want them to act like the "I"-10s they are. (See Rule #14.)
- You want them to create positive affirmations.
- You want to make sure they don't get stuck in a comfort zone.
- You want to make sure they aren't paralyzed by fear, doubt, or worry.

By the way, all four of those points apply to you, as well. Success really is between your ears. Success and failure are both true—depending on what you believe.

THE SANDLER TAKEAWAY FOR SALES LEADERS

Attitude, the second point on the Success Triangle, is simply belief.

1. Make sure all the members of your team act like the "I"-10s they are.
2. Make sure they have confidence and conviction in the company and their future.
3. Make sure they have a belief that the marketplace is one of abundance, not scarcity.

Teach Solid Technique

Emphasize tactics, strategy, and presence.

TECHNIQUE, THE THIRD part of the Success Triangle, is about skill. Specifically, it's about the tactics that support a winning strategy.

Salespeople need to have certain specific skills in order to succeed on the job. Skills turn into behavior when they're consistently executed. For instance, using LinkedIn to build relationships with new prospects with whom you haven't yet communicated. Maybe you don't know how to do that. But once you do have a process for doing that and you start executing that process consistently, it becomes a behavior. By the way, the fact that a salesperson knows a certain *skill* does not mean the salesperson is automatically going to execute that skill. Identifying the internal obstacles that keep salespeople from executing is a major objective of the coaching process. (See Rule #21.)

Each of the top ten behaviors for salespeople I shared with you in Rule #21 demands a particular skill set. A top-performing field salesperson, by definition, will have transformed each and every one of those skill sets into consistently executed behaviors. By contrast, someone who hasn't ever sold anything, hasn't been trained in any of those areas, and has no role models in professional sales would likely have gaps in each of those areas. That person would have a lot of catching up to do in terms of technique and would have to master the required skills in all ten categories.

The best approach when it comes to helping people out with this third point of the Success Triangle is to start with simple skills and to focus on those that support specific compartments of the Sandler Submarine. The first skill I would put on that particular list is one that supports every single one of those compartments. It's something that a lot of people don't even realize is a skill: personal presence.

By personal presence, I don't mean salespeople doing the job in exactly the way the manager would do it. I mean the expression of individual salespeople's distinctive personal style. I mean salespeople unlocking something that is authentic to their outlook, personality, and experience, in a unique way, and using that to interact with others. I'm talking about something that communicates personal strength and confidence, something that says, "I have a right to reach out to you as an equal because I know I have value I can add to your day." (See also the discussion on identity and role in Rule #14.)

Personal presence comes from tonality, body language, and words. Deploying it takes genuine skill, and your salespeople need that skill to work their way through the submarine at full effectiveness. If they have a good script but they sound tentative over the phone because they don't have personal presence, they do not yet have the skill of prospecting by phone—which means they can't turn it into a consistent behavior.

If you're looking for a good place to start with your salespeople, ask yourself how they rank in the area of personal presence. If there's a skill gap there, try to help them to close the gap. Personal presence usually falls into the "I know it when I see it" category, and I suspect you will. It is not all that hard to identify, discuss, and reinforce—as long as there's a respectful peer-to-peer relationship in place between you and the individual.

Be sure you help salespeople develop a strategy for learning new skills and for executing the skills they have. Don't forget to create a management playbook for yourself—one that's rooted in solid technique.

THE SANDLER TAKEAWAY FOR SALES LEADERS

Technique, the third point of the Success Triangle, is all about skill.

1. When helping salespeople with technique, start with simple skills, and focus on those that support specific compartments of the Sandler Submarine.

2. Help the salesperson develop a personal presence, meaning a distinctive personal selling style. This should not be your style. Deploying this personal presence is a core skill that supports all the compartments of the Sandler Submarine.

3. Don't forget to create a management playbook for yourself, one that's rooted in solid technique.

Create a Personalized Goals List

Set the ground rules before there's a crisis; conduct weekly individual meetings.

HAVE YOU EVER noticed this? During a job interview with salespeople, sales managers have a tendency to focus on all the positives of the role, the company, and the opportunity. They tell the salesperson, "You could make X dollars here." Or: "Here's what the benefit package looks like." Or: "Here's what the vacation time is going to be." More importantly, though, is the discussion about what the success criteria looks like and what will happen if these are not met. This is the discussion about what it takes for the salesperson to get fired from the organization. All too often, the topic is never raised.

This is also a critical discussion to have with all your existing people—not just your incoming new hires. They need to understand not only what has to happen for them to hit a home run (which sales managers are usually pretty good at talking about), but also what choices and actions on the salesperson's part would result in a decision on management's side to part company and withdraw the opportunity of employment. Typically, this means outlining what five or six elements of the success recipe if ignored or overlooked for a clearly defined period of time would lead to a serious discussion about whether there is a fit between the person and the successful execution of the role.

There are two big reasons why managers find this a particularly difficult subject to raise. First is the perceived emotional difficulty of the discussion. This is an understandable reaction. But ask yourself, when the time to let a salesperson go does come around, would you rather have it look like this decision happened because you were in a bad mood that day or because the salesperson failed to follow through on a series of agreed-upon commitments?

The second major reason that managers avoid this topic is that they themselves have never established exactly what has to happen in order for someone to be let go. That means that, when there is a problem, salespeople often have no real warning—or, at least, no warning based on their activity on the job. The manager sits the person down, grimaces, and says, "OK, I'm sorry, but we're letting you go." The salesperson says, "What? Why?" The manager says, "Well, you didn't do your job."

What does that mean, exactly? Wouldn't it be better for both sides to know, up front, exactly what "not doing the job" looks like so the salesperson has the opportunity to course-correct in time? Wouldn't it be better to schedule weekly individual meetings with the salesperson setting personalized goals, regardless of how the manager thinks things may be going? During these meetings, which you should conduct with your supervisor hat on, you can follow up on specific accountabilities and confirm that every opportunity in the salesperson's pipeline has a confirmed next step in place. (Note that weekly individual meetings are not coaching sessions.)

When you are talking about the things you want to see from the salesperson in order to ensure success, get the complete picture. Make sure you look at:

* **Behavioral goals:** These are the big-picture guidelines within which the person has to operate. You both need to know what the right behaviors are and how often the behaviors need to happen. For instance: "Send five referral letters via LinkedIn each week." Or: "Have two first conversations with C-level decision makers each day."

* **Activity goals:** This is what should happen, via the daily to-do list, on a real working day. You have to make sure the salesperson is actually doing the right things to get the job done, not wasting time.

* **Results:** This is you monitoring what actually happened. Did the person send out the five referral letters via LinkedIn? What happened as a result? How did the two first conversations each day with C-level decision makers go? What happened as a result? Benchmark the results against the rest of the team and/or your expectations. If there's an obstacle to the salesperson posting the results that should accompany the behaviors, you need to find out what the obstacle is—via good coaching discussions. (See Rule #21.)

THE SANDLER TAKEAWAY FOR SALES LEADERS

Don't take a hands-off approach to the issue of what it takes for a salesperson to part company from your team.

1. Figure out the criteria for success and the timing of the consequences for not hitting those criteria.
2. Have these discussions in private.
3. Set the ground rules before there's a crisis.

Celebrate
What People Do Well

Most managers focus on the things someone can do better—but if you focus on what people are doing well, they tend to repeat it.

PEOPLE TYPICALLY LEAVE their companies for one of two reasons: either they don't feel appreciated and respected, or they aren't being challenged to reach new levels of achievement.

Unless you take proactive steps to show, without any ambiguity, that you're personally committed to making your salespeople feel appreciated for what they do well, you are vulnerable to losing the most valuable people you recruited, supervised, trained, mentored, and coached. That's just the way things work. You've got a lot of things on your plate. You're busy. You could be losing track of the relationship. Then, you wake up one morning and realize you've spent a whole lot of time, money, and attention developing a sales-person who has just started to work for somebody else.

You can always find areas where a salesperson needs to improve. Someone could do many, many things right, and you might still focus on the one or two areas that need improvement. That's natural, and everyone does it to some extent. You need to bear in mind, though, that it's remarkably easy to get people to repeat the actions you want them to repeat. All you have to do is compliment them.

For instance: "George, I love how you always end the meetings with 'OK, let's review our next steps.' That really gets the call buttoned up!" George might have just done that once, but when you call attention to it in the form of a compliment, George will make sure he repeats it on every sales call.

You can follow up on these kinds of conversations by sending "fuzzy files" (some kind of positive, personalized reinforcement and acknowledgment) at least every 90 days and by finding opportunities to spend quality time with each team member. You will have lower turnover. You will waste a lot less time because you'll know what's operationally important to each individual on the staff. In the end, you will have a much more productive team.

THE SANDLER TAKEAWAY FOR SALES LEADERS

If there's a salesperson on your team who is worth keeping, there's also a conversation that's worth having about how you can make that person feel good about the job.

1. In a one-on-one setting, ask what the person needs from you in order to be happy in the job and to hit key goals.
2. Listen with both ears to the salesperson's response.
3. Send "fuzzy files" every 90 days, and spend quality time with each salesperson.

Your Customer Is Your Competitor's Prospect

Take part in a quarterly business review with your salespeople and their most important customers.

A QUARTERLY BUSINESS review (QBR) is a specially called meeting with you, your salespeople, and the highest-ranking people at each of their most important accounts—including, you hope, the founders or CEOs. If the business is critical to your company and if you want to maintain or increase wallet share within this account, you must schedule and attend this meeting every 90 days, and so must your salesperson.

The meeting must directly address the following five questions, from you and your salesperson to the highest-ranking people on the customer's side. Don't skip any of the questions, and don't change or water them down.

1. **"Why did you hire us?"** You must get an answer to this question, and you need to keep that answer top-of-mind with the customer. Many accounts might have forgotten why they originally brought you in, which leaves you vulnerable to the competition.

2. **"On a scale of ten (high) and one (low), how effectively are we servicing your needs?"** Understanding the customer's number and the underlying reasons behind that answer is the only the way you can improve your service levels. If you don't, there's a good chance they will eventually leave. Our experience is that the #1 reason clients leave is that they don't feel appreciated. Asking this particular question dramatically decreases the chances of this becoming an issue.

3. **"What else should we be doing for you?"** By asking how you can deliver better service for this customer, you are asking, in essence, what else you should be selling into the account. It's not uncommon for a customer to shop a competitor for some of the very products/services a current vendor provides. This question serves as an insurance policy. If you don't ask it, it's likely you won't identify opportunities to expand your business presence.

4. **"What would make you dissatisfied with our service—or even decide to fire us?"** No, you're not going to plant the idea of firing in the CEO's mind. If the seed isn't there already, this question isn't going to cause the option to be considered. If it is there, you need to know about it. The fact that a customer is buying from you right now doesn't mean you're invulnerable. You need to get the negatives out on the table for discussion. Most people are afraid of them—but that doesn't mean they don't exist. You need to uncover and learn about any brush fires that may have inadvertently been started along the way.

5. **"Who else do you know who may be struggling with the same issues we're helping you with—and would you be willing to introduce us to them?"** This is a particularly powerful request for referrals. You will get names when you ask for them. Write them all down.

Those five questions are the baseline of a good quarterly meeting. Asking those questions tends to show appreciation, solve problems before they become crises, and make relationships last longer.

Make scheduling QBRs part of your team review.

THE SANDLER TAKEAWAY FOR SALES LEADERS

QBR stands for quarterly business review. If the account is important enough for you to want to keep or expand wallet share within it, you and your salesperson must schedule a meeting, attend, and ask five key questions.

1. Don't make the assumption that because they're buying from you, they must be a good customer.

2. Ask: "Why did you hire us?" Ask: "On a scale of ten (high) and one (low), how effectively are we servicing your needs?" Ask: "What else should we be doing for you?" Ask: "What would make you dissatisfied with our service or even decide to fire us?" Ask: "Who else do you know who may be struggling with the same issues we're helping you with—and would you be willing to introduce us to them?"

3. Those five questions are the baseline of a good QBR meeting. Asking them shows appreciation, solves problems before they become crises, and makes good business relationships last longer.

RULE #40

Have a Debriefing Process

Publish your debriefing questions.

DEBRIEFING AFTER EVERY sales call is the single best way to shape your team's performance. If you have well-established questions that team members know about ahead of time, then they will gather the information needed even when you're not on the call. If you don't, they won't. It's that simple.

For most sales managers, the post-call debriefing is a lost opportunity. The typical debriefing consists of a single question, like: "How'd it go?" The salespeople say, "Great!" (Or something equally vague.) Then they share whatever they feel like sharing. End of debriefing session.

A more comprehensive debriefing strategy does several things. First and foremost, it gives you a clear picture, in real time, of what's actually happening on the sales call, and you certainly want to know about that. But debriefing can do much more than that. You can use debriefing questions to shape people's behavior on a sales call without you being there.

It's hard to be on every sales call as a sales manager. But in a sense, you could have your personal hologram sitting on their shoulders during the sales meeting—if you give salespeople a list of debriefing questions that they know you are going to ask about whenever you debrief.

Tell your salesperson: "OK. Here's the deal. I am going to ask you these ten questions at the end of every call that we talk about. That doesn't mean I am going to talk to you about every call, and it doesn't mean I am not going to ask you more than these ten questions. In fact, chances are that when I have the time, I am going to ask you 100 questions. But whenever we do talk about a sales call of yours, you can rest assured I am always going to ask you these ten questions. I need you to be able to answer them."

Now you review the ten most important issues that you know absolutely, positively have to be covered on every sales call. Do be sure you write the list up ahead of time—don't wing it—and hand each person a copy of the list. Remember that the questions must be relevant to every prospect and customer with whom your salespeople will interact. A non-negotiable question that must be on your list is: "What was the up-front contract for the call/meeting?" (See Rule #3.)

Your salesperson will probably scan the sheet and say something like, "Hmm, well, most of the time, I ask most of those questions." Be firm on this point: Asking most of those questions, most of the time, is not enough. Make sure your salespeople know they need to be able to give you the answers to all of those questions, all of the time.

Here are some additional sample "sit on your shoulder" questions you may want to include on your list:

- "What pain indicators did you uncover?"
- "What is their budget?"
- "How do they make decisions to purchase?"
- "Are there any other companies working with this prospect?"
- "What is the clear next step?"

The next time you talk to a salesperson about a sales call, take the time to ask each and every one of your ten questions. Make the salesperson color within the lines. Send the clear message: "In order to be successful, you need know this information after the first meeting with a prospect."

THE SANDLER TAKEAWAY FOR SALES LEADERS

Create a formal debriefing strategy.

1. "How'd it go?" is not a debriefing strategy.
2. Create and publish a list of ten questions the salesperson must be able to answer about each and every sales call.
3. Ask those ten issues after the completion of every sales call.

Team Selling Requires Planning

Make sure team-selling opportunities are well-choreographed.

MOST TEAM-SELLING SITUATIONS end up being three talented people winging it—each looking at the call from only their own perspective. It shouldn't be that way.

Team selling is a tremendous opportunity for you to show the breadth and depth of your company and for you to shine as a sales leader—but you have to orchestrate the performance. To do that, follow these steps.

1. Do a comprehensive pre-call planning meeting. At a minimum, 50% of your call time should be invested in a pre-call plan—therefore, a 60-minute meeting would mean at least a 30-minute pre-call planning session. That's not the same thing as chatting about the meeting in the car on your way to the location. You're investing significant resources in this opportunity—and you want to position your team to win the deal. That means a formal planning session is needed. This meeting should be set at least three days in advance of the actual meeting to allow time for

strategy adjustments, resources, and other preparation. As the sales lead, you should ensure that all details are in order. Where will you park? What are your audio-visual needs? Do you have hard copies of the materials in the event something unexpected happens technologically?

2. Match the people on the selling side with those on the buying side from a DISC behavioral standpoint. (See Rule #8.) Everyone on your team should understand the DISC styles of the key players on the buying side, and everyone should be ready to adapt to those styles or hand the ball off to someone who can.

3. Match the people on the selling side with those on the buying side from a functional perspective. Ideally, the roles and responsibilities of the people on your team should match the roles and responsibilities of the people who will be attending the meeting on the buying side. All too often, sales managers fail to even ask the question, "Who should we be bringing?" Everyone in attendance from the seller's side should have a role in the meeting.

4. Map out the sequence of the meeting. Who will set the up-front contract? What will that look like? Who will introduce people? Who will do what, when? From whom will the prospective client expect to hear? How long will each person have to talk? Determine all this ahead of time. Don't put yourself in the position where you let everyone say what everyone wants to say— and you look up at the clock and realize you have eight minutes left to cover 30 minutes' worth of material. Many presentations come off the rails due to a lack of process, structure, and understanding of each person's role in the meeting.

5. Set up some time for a post-meeting debrief. Allocate time on the calendar, before the meeting is even held, for a formal debrief session. Too often, follow up and debrief becomes a loose

conversation in the car and a few hasty emails. Put it on the calendar well in advance and hold attendees accountable for attendance. At this session, you should ask: "What did we learn?"
"What did we do well?" "What did we do not so well?" "What
are our actions moving forward, and who is doing them?" "What
are specific deadlines for getting the follow up completed?"
"Who will be the point of contact with the prospect?"

If you follow these five steps, your team-selling efforts will be far
more productive.

THE SANDLER TAKEAWAY FOR SALES LEADERS

Plan team-selling opportunities with care. Don't wing it.

1. Set up time on the calendar for a comprehensive planning meeting. Figure out who's doing what, when.
2. Spend at least half as much time preparing for the
   meeting as you will be in it.
3. Follow the five steps for planning, including setting up
   time for a post-meeting debrief.

RULE #42

Create Smart Benchmarks

When it comes to account and territory planning, make sure the short game supports the long game.

HAVE YOU EVER had the experience of sitting down with a salesperson in January, setting up clear, realistic, and exciting goals for a particular current account—and then finding in August or September or October that you are nowhere near the attainment of that goal? Of course, you have. All managers have. The question is, why does that happen?

Very often, it's because the managers didn't set up the right calendar benchmarks. They only set a yearly goal. This is a critical mistake many managers make in the area of account and territory planning.

Account plans that are set up for your team's territories and the accounts within those territories shouldn't have a single annual goal. You have to break those goals down into the equivalent 90-day goals, and you need to get buy-in from each salesperson on each individual 90-day goal that supports the big annual goal. Otherwise, your short-term game won't support your long-term strategy for the account.

A goal that's supposed to be attained over a one-year period may seem plausible when you're punching numbers into the spreadsheet.

But if you're honest and you look closely at the team's history, you'll realize that the annual plan for that account often has nothing to do with the salesperson's activity in real time. You need to do a reality check in these situations. Just typing in another annual goal is not going to get the job done, and neither is blaming the salesperson.

If you want your people's account plans to be followed and if you want real accountability, you need to set up 90-day account plans with your sales force. These plans should, of course, support the annual goal for the account or territory.

Look at the case notes together. Talk about what the salesperson plans to do over the next three months to deepen the relationships and increase your wallet share within the account. Repeat this process every quarter.

By setting and focusing on 90-day goals, your salesperson will be much more likely to look back on a 12-month period and say, "Wow, I've really accomplished something here." The key is to set and get personal commitments for short-term goals. That's particularly essential within current accounts where your goal is to maintain and deepen existing relationships. Remember, your current customer is somebody else's prospect. (See also Rule #30.) Use the KARE system to figure out what level of KARE you will be providing, to whom and how, over the next 90 days.

THE SANDLER TAKEAWAY FOR SALES LEADERS

Set and win buy-in on 90-day goals in account and territory planning.

1. Build individual quarterly plans together with your salespeople.
2. These goals should support your annual objectives for their accounts or territory.
3. Use the KARE system (Rule #30) to figure out what level of KARE you will be providing, to whom and how, over the next 90 days.

Track the Leading Indicators

Forecast effectively.

THERE'S A BIG difference between effective and ineffective sales forecasting. Most of the complaints we at Sandler hear from sales managers connect to the latter.

Ineffective sales forecasting is what happens when you go to a salesperson and say, "Maya, give me a number that forecasts your closed deals over the next 90 days." Maya says, "OK. $200,000." Ninety days later, it turns out $200,000 wasn't even close. That's the scenario managers tend to complain to us about.

The problem is that the number you're asking Maya to provide—total closed sales three months from now—is typically not predictable. She literally doesn't know what's going to happen and has no process for even making an educated guess. It's not that surprising that the estimates salespeople share don't always come close.

Here's a more effective way to create a forecast. Draw two lines down the center of a piece of paper, making three columns. In the left column, identify the top five behaviors that impact the forecast.

Top Five Impact Behaviors	Weekly KPIs (Goals)	Weekly KPIs (Actual)
1. Prospecting		
—Cold Calls	75	60
—Bus. Intros	5	3
2. First Face-to-Face Meetings	6	4
3. Qualified Proposals	2	2
4. Meetings to present products to existing clients	2	2
5. Close the sale or Close the file meetings	2	1

In the middle column, put the numbers you want the salesperson to hit each week in each of those five behavior areas. These are the key performance indicator (KPI) targets you want to see turn into reality, week after week.

In the rightmost column, track what the salesperson is actually doing in each of these areas. These are the real-world numbers the person posts over time in all five behavior areas.

Keep this up every week for, say, six weeks. Then look at the person's numbers and at the sales actually closed over that timeframe. You now know whether the salesperson is performing above or below the KPIs you've identified, and you know what actual revenue that level of activity brought in. Then you (not the salesperson) can extrapolate out what the revenue from that same activity level is likely to be 90 days from now.

Your forecast for the salesperson should be based on the real-world data you now have in front of you and on the trends you can project if the KPI levels you've tracked and recorded continue at their current pace. That will give you a better, more reliable number.

(By the way, I've said to do this on a sheet of paper to make it easy for you to visualize, but of course you can record these figures on a spreadsheet as well.)

Here's an example of the kind of thing you should be looking out for when you're monitoring Maya's numbers and trying to forecast income from her performance. Prospecting is a behavior you expect Maya to perform on a weekly basis. A KPI for prospecting would be the actual number of first face-to-face appointments yielded by the performance of the behavior. Six first face-to-face or voice-to-voice meetings per week might be an indicator of acceptable behavioral performance if it supports the amount of revenue you want her to bring in. If that's the case, six per week could be identified as the KPI of success in this area—the number that supports Maya's income goal. If Maya only delivers three first face-to-face meetings in a given week, she would therefore be performing below KPI—and that's going to affect your income forecast for her.

Track and forecast the behaviors—they are predictable. You can count how many times Maya actually does them, and you can confirm whether she is on track, day after day, week after week, and month after month. Most sales managers only focus on the final number, the number that defines revenue. They leave out everything that leads up to that.

There's a reason that numbers defining actual closed deals are called "lagging indicators." Yes, they're important because they're revenue, but you always have to remind yourself that they're the result of other things that the salesperson does. Behaviors are the leading indicators. Those are what predict success. If you track the behaviors first and then look at this salesperson's history to see what the trends are, you'll get a much more accurate and meaningful selection of data—and you'll be able to make better estimates about what's likely to happen in terms of revenue.

The big questions in terms of forecasting are:

- Do you have the right salespeople?
- Do you have the right behaviors to measure?
- Are the salespeople posting the right number of KPIs to support their income goal?

Effective sales forecasting is essential. It helps you figure out where people are in the process and what it's going to take for them to make progress. It's vitally important that, as a manager, you have a clear set of expectations with your team about what needs to be reported in order for good sales forecasting to happen. For instance, you need to understand what kinds of up-front contracts are actually in place during an initial meeting, and you and the team need to agree on which two or three steps need to be completed before accounts move to the next step in the sales process. (See Rule #1.) This type of discipline will improve your team's forecasting accuracy.

THE SANDLER TAKEAWAY FOR SALES LEADERS

Don't make people guess about their future income totals. Track and forecast their behaviors. Then generate income projections based on those behavior numbers.

1. Most sales managers only focus on the final number, the number that defines revenue. They leave out everything that leads up to the closed sale.

2. Numbers defining actual closed deals are lagging indicators. They're the result of other things the salesperson does. Behaviors are leading indicators. They're more meaningful because they actually predict success.

3. Have an agreed-upon sales process; make sure the team understands the steps that have to happen before an opportunity proceeds to the next step.

Create a Proactive Approach to Social Selling

Drill the three-point shot.

SOCIAL SELLING, THE latest addition to the professional sales team's arsenal of weapons involving online networking tools, doesn't fundamentally change the way your team prospects and sells—but it does have the potential to change the strategy of their game. In fact, it can revolutionize that strategy, just like the introduction of the three-point line did for professional basketball.

For many years, there was no such thing as a three-point shot in American basketball. Then, in the 1960s, scoring three points from a new line added to the court was introduced to "give the smaller player a chance to score and open up the defense to make the game more enjoyable for the fans," according to George Mikan, commissioner of the American Basketball Association. When the three-point shot became a reality, there was suddenly a whole new dynamic—a different way to pursue the same basic goal of outscoring the other team.

A line drawn on the court won't necessarily change the way you take your shot. What it will do, though, is change where you shoot from, how you score more points, and how you manage the risk of shooting from farther away. Social selling is revolutionizing prospecting in many of the same ways.

If members of your team are already getting enough slam-dunk leads with what they're doing right now, they probably don't care much about learning that trickier outside shot (though they should at least have a working knowledge of the tactics). However, if other team members have been constantly, desperately firing off the sales equivalent of desperate half-court shots, working on improving those people's social-selling skills is probably a good idea. If a salesperson on your staff is somewhere in between those two extremes and is already making difficult cold calls or walk-in prospecting calls, it might make sense to help that individual learn how to use today's social-selling tools to put up a few extra points. (There is a generational factor to consider here, too; younger salespeople are, as a general rule, more receptive to the idea of mastering social-selling skills than older members of the team.)

It is important to remember, though, that the fundamentals of prospecting and selling haven't changed because you now have LinkedIn—just like the proper form for shooting a basketball hasn't changed in 100 years or so. You still have to manage your own time effectively. (We advise salespeople to spend a maximum of 30 minutes on LinkedIn each business day.) The point is, there are abundant new tools, tactics, and strategies available for communication, research, and referrals that you can now use to execute your sales strategy in new, exciting, and more effective ways.

There are many activities for identifying prospective clients using today's interactive communication technologies, and all of them overlap to some degree. We broadly classify these activities into two categories: passive and proactive. Social-selling activities are an important part of your team's prospecting arsenal—but you have to be sure to put the emphasis on (and measure) the proactive activities.

Passive tactics include things like following someone else's discussion thread without commenting or checking who is following your personal account on Twitter. Those may be interesting and even important things for your team members to do occasionally, but they won't directly result in any interactions with other people. They're basically about observing outside events.

Proactive, or hands-on, social-selling activities engage with others using a tactic over which the salesperson has control. So for instance, sending messages requesting referrals to second-degree connections on LinkedIn, posting articles, and following up with existing accounts via email are all proactive endeavors. These are all activities that connect your salespeople to interactions with other people and that they can control. The salespeople cannot necessarily control the outcome of the activity, but they can control whether or not the activity takes place, and you can measure how often the salesperson does it.

Here's the key concept to bear in mind when it comes to social selling: You can't manage something you can't control. Posting a status update on LinkedIn and waiting for someone to comment on it is more passive and out of your control than researching an ideal prospect and sending that person an InMail message to start a conversation. You want the actions to be the salesperson's responsibility.

Here are ten proactive ways your team can use social selling to prospect more effectively:

1. Search the connections of your meetings ahead of time and bring five names to ask for referrals.
2. Create a saved search of prospects in LinkedIn's advanced search of about ten times the number of sales you need in a year, and pursue introductions.

3. Pay attention to your "likes," comments, and people who viewed your profile, and then reach out to start conversations.

4. Check "people also viewed" and "similar companies" on LinkedIn whenever you bring on a new client. That way, you can pursue the same kind of prospect.

5. Schedule and send educational posts to specific suspects, prospects, and strategic alliances to spur conversations.

6. Write long-form blog posts, share them with groups and target prospects, and then follow up to get feedback and start a conversation. Position yourself as a thought leader within your area of expertise.

7. Send InMail requests to your first-degree contacts for an introduction to those of their contacts you're trying to reach in situations where you can't get a warm introduction.

8. Don't be afraid to pick up the telephone or take the conversation offline when you see a buying signal online.

9. Research offline leads and prospects on LinkedIn to find specific conversation starters. Keep in touch through birthdays, work anniversaries, and especially job changes.

10. Be active in your updates. Post meaningful information regularly.

Notice that all of these activities can be measured over time and tracked for effectiveness.

Many salespeople have found that proactive actions like these can help them to find prospects, heat up cold calls, and bring valuable introductions or information to the sales process. They use sites like LinkedIn to search for decision makers, research ideal clients or companies, and identify new opportunities—making it significantly easier to find and interact with the right prospect. They have learned, with a little practice, how to sink the three-point shot.

Social selling is the three-point line of prospecting. It's a small change in strategy that is delivering better results for many salespeople, and it is revolutionizing the way the game is being played. But your team still has to practice. They still have to hustle, and they still have to take their best shots in order to become the best players they can be. A big part of that effort will be sustaining what we call a "personal connection" interaction philosophy. If salespeople happen to have a good call or meeting with a buyer, they should make a point of connecting with that person on LinkedIn. If your salesperson is trying to get the attention of particular buyers, then following those people and commenting on their posts may be a good first stage in connecting. The point is not to amass huge numbers of contacts, as though the salesperson were collecting baseball cards, but to be actively trying to connect with decision makers online in a thoughtful and strategic manner.

THE SANDLER TAKEAWAY FOR SALES LEADERS

The key concept to bear in mind when it comes to social selling is that you can't manage what you can't control.

1. Encourage proactive approaches to social selling—have a goal for introductions each month.
2. Don't spend more than 30 minutes on LinkedIn per day.
3. Track everything.

Your Job Doesn't End When They're Hired

Create good onboarding to ensure success; conduct exit interviews.

EFFECTIVELY ONBOARDING NEW employees is one of the most important things you can do in order to increase the odds of a successful jumpstart for a new hire. Yet it is usually low on the priority list.

Most managers spend a large amount of time, effort, and energy looking for an applicant. The interview process is relatively short and the onboarding process is non-existent. Typically, people are welcomed into the company and then asked to spend time with a seasoned veteran who is supposed to "show them the ropes." Experience has shown that, on its own, this is not an effective onboarding process.

How long does it take a new hire, on average, to be profitable in your company? Do you know? Do you track it? Can you improve upon it? Do you know if an individual new hire is doing better or worse than the company average? If you don't track the number, then you can't improve upon it.

I believe you can reduce the time from hire to profitability by 50% if you follow these three steps:

1. Create a list of all of the things that people have to do in order to be successful at the job. The job offers have been made. New employees want to be successful, and the company wants them to be successful. Take full advantage of that shared objective. Give them a list of activities essential to success at your organization. For instance: Each person should have a great elevator pitch (also known as a 30-second commercial), should be able to list and discuss the major competitors in the marketplace, should be able to set a good up-front contract (see Rule #3), and should be able to answer ten specific, predictable questions from you after an initial sales call (see Rule #40). That's just a start. You must, of course, customize this list to your situation and market.

2. Give your new people good examples of everything you've listed. For instance, include a sample 30-second commercial, ideally in both audio and written form. Do that for everything you've given them in the first step. Give them an overview of the competitive landscape, and so on. Take the best examples you have from your team. Using examples from specific team members will dramatically improve adoption of these best practices.

3. Give your new people a date by which all that material should be known and owned. For instance, you might set the expectation that each has a great 30-second commercial to deliver by the end of the second week. Do that for everything on the list, and get clear agreements from new hires that they will demonstrate mastery and delivery by each date.

Do those three things, and you will dramatically reduce the learning curve for your new hires.

Just as essential as the onboarding process, and even more consistently ignored, is the offboarding process. This is particularly important for sales teams experiencing unacceptably high turnover rates. If you can, schedule private, one-on-one exit interviews with salespeople who have decided to move on to other opportunities. Ask what you could have done to improve the experience of working on your team. Ask why the person is leaving (especially if you think you already know). Listen with both ears. If you are consistently losing the good people you hire, develop, supervise, train, mentor, and coach, you need to know what's behind that phenomenon. If you keep hearing the same answers from different people, develop a strategy for constructive change.

THE SANDLER TAKEAWAY FOR SALES LEADERS

Onboarding processes are essential, but routinely overlooked.

1. Create a list of everything people have to do in order to be successful at the job. Share this list with new hires. Give them a date by which all that material should be owned.
2. Doing this will reduce the time from hire to profitability by 50%.
3. Conduct exit interviews with salespeople who decide to leave your team.

Reward the Behavior You Want to Increase

Build smart compensation plans.

MOST COMPENSATION PLANS are designed to pay an individual a certain amount of money—not necessarily to achieve a certain goal.

That's a mistake. A salesperson's compensation plan has to be aligned with the sales team's objectives. If the person is a hunter tasked with tracking down brand new customers, the plan should be heavily weighted toward commissions and should reward finding new pieces of business. What we at Sandler find with most commission plans, though, is that while management wants their people to hunt, they're paying them to farm.

If the goal is to have 70% of revenue coming from new accounts and 30% coming from existing growth, your compensation scheme had better align with those numbers and be heavily weighted toward acquiring new business. If it's not, if it's weighted in a different direction for the sole reason that that's "what we've always done," there's likely to be a problem.

Here's what I'm talking about.

Manager Maurice tells his salesperson Shavone that he wants her to go out and contribute as a hunter. Maurice says, "Shavone, you're going to get a base pay of $45,000 and 20% commission on everything you sell, regardless of whether it's a new client or an existing client."

What does Shavone do? She goes right out and takes meticulous care of the clients she already has. She's not motivated to go out and find new business.

But if Maurice sets up a plan that says to Shavone, "OK, you're going to make slightly less in base pay—$40,000—but you're going to make a 25% commission on all your new business and you're going to earn a 15% commission on your recurring business." That's alignment with the team's goals.

Shavone does the math. Next thing you know, she's bringing in new clients regularly.

Invest a little time to take a good hard look at your compensation plan. Make sure the program matches your goals.

THE SANDLER TAKEAWAY FOR SALES LEADERS

The compensation structure has to be keyed to the goals of the sales team.

1. Closely review each salesperson's compensation plan.
2. If the person is a hunter tasked with tracking down brand new customers, the plan should be heavily weighted toward commissions and reward finding new pieces of business.
3. The same basic principle applies to farmers that you want to motivate. The plan you set up for them should directly reward them for expanding business within existing accounts.

Be a Role Model for Effective Time Management

Walk your talk.

EFFECTIVE TIME MANAGEMENT is a critical attribute for anyone who aspires to be a successful leader. The stakes here are higher for sales leaders than they are for other managers, though. This is because salespeople tend to take their time-management cues from their manager—and poor time-management skills tend to have a ripple effect that affect the income, and thus the viability, of the entire enterprise.

Most managers we talk to complain that there are not enough hours in the day. They fall behind in their administrative responsibilities, they do their best to catch up, and one day it dawns on them: They have become reactive paper pushers, as opposed to proactive people developers. They know their working day is out of balance. Not only that, they know the team's working day is similarly out of balance. They tell their salespeople to do a better job of prioritizing, while they themselves aren't that great at it. They know they're not walking their talk.

It would be great to be able to tap a button on a smartphone and download a few extra hours into the day, but unfortunately, there's no app for that. Managers themselves need to figure out how to restructure their time so they can a) be more effective and b) serve as a better role model for their sales team.

Assume a 40-hour work week and two weeks off for vacation, and you realize you've only got about 2,000 hours of work time to manage over a given year. That's not a lot of time. Start by thinking about how you can make the best possible investment for where you will spend those 2,000 hours. In order to maximize your efficiency, you need to make smarter investment choices with each and every one of those precious hours. The question is, how do you do that?

Ask yourself: "What are some current activities on which I could stop spending my precious working hours?"

For instance, does it ever happen that you're expected to drop everything the moment salespeople walk into your office—with zero notice ahead of time—to deal with a problem that they want you to solve?

Be honest. The answer is, "Yes." As it happens, Sandler has found that dealing with this situation more effectively is the #1 rapid improvement strategy for poor time-investment choices among sales managers with whom we work. Let's begin here.

If you have gotten into the habit of taking over the steering wheel every single time a salesperson feels like rolling down the window, unbuckling the seatbelt, and leaping from a speeding car, let me challenge you now to start thinking about ways that you can change that habit. Changing any habit takes time, of course, but changing this one is a particularly high priority for both you and the team. It's one I would urge you to begin dealing with right away.

If your response when the salesperson walks into your office saying with some variation on "Fix this!" is a knee-jerk "Sure, what can I do?," I want you to consider saying something like this instead:

"Vien, I'd love to help you, but could you come back to me in 30 minutes? Between now and then, would you be nice enough to think about two or three ways that you would suggest we solve this problem?"

If you've gotten into the habit of bailing your salespeople out of any and every challenge, you will find that saying this is going to take practice. So practice. Say this out loud a couple of times, in private, before you try it during the working day. Once you do say it, it's going to constitute a pattern interrupt so you should expect a surprised expression and possibly a little pushback. It is absolutely imperative that you stand your ground, politely, with the salesperson.

Doing so helps both you and the salesperson. You will win back precious time in your own day. You'll be a much better role model when it comes to prioritization and time management, and the salesperson will learn to become more self-sufficient.

Once you've started walking your talk when it comes to your time management, you can feel better about asking your team members to look more critically at their own time investments. A great place to start is with the concept of pay time.

1. **Pay time** activities are those that have a direct impact on your salesperson's income and your company's performance: prospecting, appointments, service calls, and so on.

2. **No-pay time** activities are those that do not lead directly to the salesperson's ability to make a trip to the bank, such as planning, administration, marketing promotions, following discussion threads online, and cleaning the office.

Activities that happen during no-pay time may be counterproductive, but they are sometimes necessary. However, the more pay-time activities your salespeople schedule and execute, the greater their sales efficiency.

Below, you will find a Pay Time/No-Pay Time worksheet that will help your team members to plan an effective selling day—and stay on the right sight of the trouble line.

PAY TIME/NO-PAY TIME WORKSHEET

Sandler Rule: Stay on the right side of the trouble line.

No-Pay Time	Pay Time
My no-pay time is:	My pay time is:
(ex. 7 A.M. to 8 A.M., lunch, 5 P.M. to 6 P.M.)	(ex. 8 A.M. to 12 P.M. and 1 P.M. to 5 P.M.)
Activities:	Activities:

TROUBLE LINE

Examples of no-pay-time activities:
- Reading emails and product info
- Working on marketing promotions or customer service surveys
- Completing reports and paperwork
- Goal setting and planning

Examples of pay-time activities:
- Prospecting
- Scheduled appointments with prospects and customers
- Service calls
- Following up on referrals

THE SANDLER TAKEAWAY FOR SALES LEADERS

Walk your talk when it comes to time management.

1. Consider that you only have 2,000 working hours to invest in a given year. Each and every one of those hours is precious and should be treated accordingly.

2. When salespeople walk into your office unannounced and expect you to solve a problem for them, consider saying something like: "I'd love to help you, but could you come back to me in 30 minutes? Between now and then, would you be nice enough to think about two or three ways that you would suggest we solve this problem?"

3. Share the Pay Time/No-Pay Time worksheet with your team members.

Don't Expect Sustainable Change from a Single Event

Understand how your salespeople learn and grow.

DAVID SANDLER FAMOUSLY pointed out that you can't teach a kid to ride a bicycle at a seminar. He was pointing out the futility of expecting lasting behavioral change from a single training event. It just doesn't work that way. Training and development is not a one-time fix. It's not a rally to which you send people. It's not something you check off and consider finished. It's a long-term commitment to each individual's unique growth as a person. It goes on indefinitely.

Adults learn in three ways: by interacting with a trainer or teacher, by engaging with course material, and by socializing with their peer group. That's where all sustainable learning comes from—those three sources. The more consistently and the longer you have them in play, the more sustainable the learning is.

If you execute a learning and development initiative properly, what happens is that those three elements combine. They bond the group over time, making learning part of the team's culture. In this situation, which is the one we at Sandler work to bring about not just on sales teams but throughout entire organizations, training is no longer an event. It's a process in which those three elements are continuously acted on and improved upon. It's how our client companies themselves operate.

As a manager who is responsible for short-term performance, you may be tempted to shy away from long-term commitments like this. You may be tempted to say, "Listen, I just want the result. I want to send the team to a seminar. I want to point them toward a high-energy weekend, and I want them to come back trained. I want them psyched, I want them knowing exactly what they need to know, and I want to knock this thing called 'training' off my list of things to do."

The questions you have to ask are: Does that approach support learning? Does it support the team? Does it improve your numbers?

Think about the last time you went to a seminar. If you're like most people, within two weeks of that seminar you had either forgotten most of what you learned or you had questions about the material that no one was there to answer. What happened then? You reverted back to your old ways of doing things. There was no meaningful change in behavior. Is that the system you want to replicate?

Here's the reality. If you manage a sales team, you need a long-term plan. You need a roadmap. That roadmap has to have mile-markers on it.

That's what we at Sandler specialize in. We help managers create a plan that says, "Over the next 12 months, here's what the team will be learning. Here's the skill, here's the knowledge, and here's the application. Guess what? You're going to be learning in a number of complementary tactics. You're going to learn by coming to class and interacting with the trainer. You're going to learn by going out and executing the models we'll be looking at together. When you come back, you're going to work with a group of your peers to see what their struggles are so you can incorporate their learning into your world—and you can make sustainable positive changes in behavior and performance."

What we do at Sandler Training is not quick. It's not cheap. It's not for everyone. But it does have one big advantage. It works.

THE SANDLER TAKEAWAY FOR SALES LEADERS

Training/development is not a one-time fix.

1. Training is a long-term commitment to each individual's unique growth as a person.

2. If you manage a sales team, you need a long-term plan that delivers sustainable positive changes in behavior and performance.

3. We at Sandler specialize in helping you set up and execute that plan.

Don't Go It Alone

Continue the journey.

HERE'S WHAT WE know: Your salespeople need you. If they are going to grow within their roles as salespeople, they need your support as a supervisor, as a trainer, as a mentor, and as a coach.

By the same token, you need someone to support you as you move forward in your career. In order to do the best possible job in helping your team to grow, you need to invest in your own personal and professional growth.

That means committing to being a lifetime learner. It also means reaching out to get guidance and support in putting into practice what you've learned in this book. Just knowing what you now know is not enough. You should commit to six to eight hours per month of learning. This could take any number of forms: reading a business book, attending training programs, or watching a video that expands a critical skill set.

If you've familiarized yourself with the Sandler Success Triangle (see Rule #33), you know that success is dependent upon three elements: behavior, attitude, and technique. Reading this book gave you exposure to a lot of great techniques. However, only working with a trained Sandler coach will enable you to activate what you've learned by making meaningful positive changes in your attitude (your beliefs about yourself, your company, your market, and your team) and your behavior (the muscle memory that drives what you do, each and every day.)

As I close this book, I invite you to take the next step by reaching out to your local Sandler office. Learn more about our live management and coaching programs. They can take you—and your team—to the next level, the level where you're not only improving your performance as a sales professional, but also coming closer to realizing your full potential as a human being.

We at Sandler believe working on who you are is just as important as working on what you do. We also believe this kind of holistic approach is the key to all lasting success in management—and indeed to success in life. We hope to speak to you soon as your partner in securing that success. You'll find your personal invitation on the final page of this book.

THE SANDLER TAKEAWAY FOR SALES LEADERS

Don't stop here. Reach out to your local Sandler trainer, and continue the journey. Visit us at www.sandler.com.

Online Access to Free Sandler Management Tools

Visit us at **www.sandler.com/management-rules-tools** for access to the following Sandler Management Tools referenced in this book.

- Rule #1: Gate Selling Tool
- Rule #3: Up-Front Contract Tool
- Rule #8: DISC Tool
- Rule #9: SEARCH Tool
- Rule #11: Cookbook for Success Tool
- Rule #15: Goals Tool
- Rule #21: The Top Ten Behaviors Tool
- Rule #24: RACI Tool

Look for these other books
on shop.sandler.com:

Prospect the Sandler Way

Transforming Leaders the Sandler Way

Selling Professional Services the Sandler Way

Accountability the Sandler Way

Selling Technology the Sandler Way

LinkedIn the Sandler Way

Bootstrap Selling the Sandler Way

Customer Service the Sandler Way

Selling to Homeowners the Sandler Way

Succeed the Sandler Way

The Contrarian Salesperson

The Sales Coach's Playbook

Lead When You Dance

Change the Sandler Way

Motivational Management the Sandler Way

Call Center Success the Sandler Way

CRASH A CLASS AND EXPERIENCE THE

POWER OF SANDLER

YOU HAVE NOTHING TO LOSE AND EVERYTHING TO GAIN.

Are you a **salesperson** who...

- Feels uneasy about the lack of qualified prospects in your pipeline?
- Spends too much time developing proposals that do not turn into business?
- Wastes time with unqualified prospects?
- Continues to get 'think-it-overs' instead of closing?

Are you a **sales leader** who...

- Is frustrated with managing a sales force that's not meeting goals?
- Is tired of hiring salespeople that won't prospect?

Expand your reach and success by attending a complimentary training session at a local Sandler office near you.

REASONS TO
CRASH A CLASS

- Improve your current processes.
- Go "beyond the book" and witness an interactive, in-person approach to a small group training.
- Discover a workable, ground-level solution.

Contact a Sandler trainer to reserve your seat today.
www.sandler.com/CRASH-A-CLASS